Ireland

Ireland

TERRY DEARY

Illustrated by Martin Brown

SCHOLASTIC

To John Tracy – the greatest living Irishman.

Scholastic Children's Books,
Commonwealth House, 1–19 New Oxford Street
London WC1A 1NU, UK

A division of Scholastic Ltd
London ~ New York ~ Toronto ~ Sydney ~ Auckland
Mexico City ~ New Delhi ~ Hong Kong

Published in the UK by Scholastic Ltd, 2000

Text copyright © Terry Deary, 2000
Illustrations copyright © Martin Brown, 2000

ISBN 0 439 01436 0

contents

Introduction

History can be horrible … but especially history that looks at the quaint and the cruel ways that humans have behaved. Of course that's what readers enjoy – look at today's newspapers. You'll see stories like …

BOY FALLS FROM CLASSROOM WINDOW, LANDS ON HEAD TEACHER AND KILLS HER!

You don't get happy stories like …

GIRL CELEBRATES HAPPY BIRTHDAY WITH TOP MARKS IN HER SATs!

Some historians are especially nasty when it comes to writing certain histories. Take the history of Ireland, for example. An Irish writer, Geoffrey Keating, once complained about English historians who loved writing horrible histories of Ireland ...

> *The English historian is like a dung beetle. He ignores the garden flowers and the sweet-smelling blossom. Instead he keeps bustling about until he meets the dung of a cow or a horse and starts to roll about in it.*

The shocking thing is that Mr Keating wasn't talking about *this* Horrible History of Ireland – he was writing almost 400 years ago! So people have been writing about the ugly side of Irish history for at least that long. And what do we have here? What are you reading? *Another* hideous and hateful history of the lovely island of Ireland.

Now Geoffrey Keating suffered for writing about English dung-beetle historians – he's said to have been killed by an English soldier of Oliver Cromwell in 1650.

KILLED FOR COMPLAINING ABOUT HISTORY BOOKS! WHAT HAPPENS IF I WANT TO COMPLAIN ABOUT THIS BOOK?

Don't worry! It's safe to say anything you like about this Horrible History and its author. Just relax and enjoy reading about the most fascinating thing of all: people and the way they behaved in the past.

OLD IRELAND

Invaders, invaders, invaders. People kept arriving in Ireland and giving the earlier ones a hard time. Yet it's a strange fact that the Irish probably did more damage to one another than all the invaders of the early Middle Ages. The Vikings were famous for robbing and burning the great monasteries, but local Irish lords plundered far more!

Old Ireland timeline

8000 BC Humans arrive in Ireland from Europe to hunt and fish. But they do not open fish shops because chips haven't been invented.

4000 BC 'Gaels' arrive in Ireland (or so the legends say). 'Gaels' were farmers … so what were the farmers' wives called? Gals?

2500 BC Stone Age Irish build Newgrange monument. Not as flashy as Stonehenge but very clever.

300 BC The Celts arrive and will rule for more than a thousand years. Fierce warriors who fight with no clothes on. That would really put the enemy off, wouldn't it?

AD 431 The Pope sends the first Irish bishop, Palladius. Of course poor Palladius is forgotten because …

432 Saint Patrick arrives from Britain and single-handedly converts Ireland to Christianity (they say). He can't have stopped to sleep or eat if that's true! But he certainly stopped in 461, when he dropped down dead.

9

664 Great plague ravages Ireland. This is good practice for all the other horrors that the Irish are going to suffer in their history.

718 War between two great monasteries – Clonmacnois and Durrow – in which 200 are killed. Monks mash monks! So much for men of peace – more like men in pieces.

795 The Vikings are coming. They'll rob and destroy the country but especially pick on the poor monks who can't fight against real warriors. Even with God on their side. The Vikings set up the new city of Dublin.

844 Irish king, Fedelmid, is robbing and wrecking more monks than the Vikings. But the monks fight back and kill him. God must have chipped in to help.

851 Vikings from Denmark arrive in Dublin and attack the Vikings from Norway who are already there. The Irish join in and help wipe out any Vikings they can! This is not a safe time or place to live, as you can see.

1014 Blood rains from the sky, soldiers are attacked by spears that fly out of walls and by ravens with iron beaks. (That's what horrible historians of the time say.) In an Irish v. Viking battle at Clontarf the Irish King Brian Boruma wins … but is killed before he can be king of all Ireland.

Cut-throat Celts

The Celts were a group of tribes who shared the same language and the same habits. (Some of those habits could be very nasty indeed, as you'll see.)

In 386 BC they'd been strong enough to attack Rome and give the Romans a rotten time. But once the Romans had got their act together (and got their army together) the Celts were pushed back and back and back till they reached Ireland.

The Celts were fierce and fearless fighters. If you want to be a feared foe, then follow these five foul steps to fame. (Try these terrible tricks today and you'll end up in prison, of course, but you may enjoy it more than maths lessons.)

1 Get yourself dressed
You need a torc. Pop down to your local jeweller's shop and ask for one. It's a metal band (usually solid gold) that you wear around your neck or your arm. It is carved with signs that will bring you luck in battle.

Apart from the torc, what else do you wear as a Celt warrior?

Nothing. Not a stitch – not even a pair of Y-fronts, a fig leaf or a bit of string to tie down your floppy bits when you run. Nothing. Your nakedness will bring you protection from the gods (Celt warriors believe) so don't worry.

DOES THAT MEAN I'LL BE PROTECTED IN THE BATH?

Not only does your nakedness get you heavenly blessing. It probably also puts the enemy off!

2 Get yourself a horse

Celtic warriors rode into battle on a two-wheeled chariot pulled by a horse. Horses were very important to the Irish Celts. Horses were raced. Horses were eaten. Horses were even worshipped – we get the name 'pony' from the Celtic and Roman horse goddess Epona.

Your horse should be fast and strong because your life could depend on it. So pick yourself a good one …

3 Get yourself a driver

Celts didn't ride into battle, steering the horse with one hand and trying to fight with the other. They had a chauffeur …

The driver dropped off his passenger and the warrior ran into the battle to fight. The driver then had to hang around and watch his boss. If the warrior got into trouble then the driver would race into the battle and pick him up again.

4 Get yourself a cart

The Celt chariots had to be tough things. Part of the terror tactics of war was to bang your weapons hard against the side of the chariot as you jump down and charge into battle. The fearful row you made would scare the enemy and make you feel brave … like today's football supporters roaring to encourage their own team and scare the opposition. The more noise you can make the better!

After the battle, the Celts had the charming habit of cutting off the heads of the enemies they had killed. Roman writers said the Celts fastened the heads on to their chariots as they rode home. But we don't know *how* they fastened the heads on!

You may have to think this through before you go into battle – will you be tying them on with bits of string? Hooking them on with sharp hooks? Nailing them on with a hammer and nails?

The dead heads have to be taken home and nailed up over your front door to show the neighbours what a hero you are.

5 Get yourself some weapons

First you need a spear. A simple javelin with a metal point. You throw that first as soon as you get in range of the enemy. Then you leap down and use your sword.

No. A strong sword is needed in battle and a fancy sword is needed in ceremonies. Get one of each. The fancy sword can then be buried alongside you if you are killed in battle! Cheerful thought, eh? By the way, make sure that the battle sword is sharp. After all, if you are defeated in battle you will be expected to use it to stab yourself.

The fancy sword may also be thrown into a lake or river when you die. That was an old Irish custom and it's told in the stories of the ancient Irish heroes. This is probably where we get the story of King Arthur's sword being thrown to the Lady of the Lake.

Of course you have to hope you don't meet one of these heroes in battle. They cheated just a bit … a big bit! One legendary hero, Fergus, had a sword as long as a rainbow that could slice the tops off hills!

The Celt warriors were fierce and brave and strong. But the Romans had something the Celts never had … teamwork. Each Celt fought for himself and his own glory – each Roman fought for the army and for Rome. In the end the boring Romans beat the cool Celts. (Fergus and his rainbow sword must have been on holiday that month.)

That's life.

Awful ancients

The tales of ancient Ireland were never written down at the time. The ancient Celts didn't go for the idea of writing – a bit like some people in your class, probably. But the old stories could still have some truth in them, because they were remembered, word for word, and passed down as long, spoken poems.

Performing poets (or 'bards') trained for up to 12 years to learn around 250 main stories. Sounds a long time but it's no more than pupils spend at school these days.

Here are two of their terrible tales ... and there may just be some truth behind them ...

Tigernmas the tartan torturing twit (919 BC)

King Tigernmas not only started the mining of gold and silver during his reign. He also brought in the wearing of coloured clothing ... tartan. (Yes, I know the Scots *think* they invented tartan. Don't tell them it was the weavers of Tigernmas or they'll get upset!) The more colours you had in your cloth then the higher you were in the Irish world. King Tigernmas must have looked like a ruling rainbow!

Anyway, you don't want to hear about the colour of his clothes, you want to hear about the colour he liked to splash about – blood red. Because the name Tigernmas means 'Lord of Death'.

He ignored the peaceful druid worship of nature and water and trees. Instead, Tigernmas brought to Ireland the worship of Cromm Cruach – the Bloody Crescent. On the Feast of Samhain (31 October, or Hallowe'en to us) old Tigernmas liked nothing better than a bit of human sacrifice to Cromm Cruach. Blood all over the place. But then the followers of Tigernmas got a bit carried away one horrific Hallowe'en and killed him!

(It's hard to feel sorry for the tartan twit, isn't it?) And Ireland went back to the watery ways of their fluid druids.

Labraid Loinseach of Leinster's lousy life (268 BC)
Labraid's dad was murdered by wicked uncle Cobhthatch. Poor little Labraid didn't get his father's throne … but he did get his father's heart. Cruel Cobhthatch made him eat it!

(Don't try this at home ... though dads' hearts can be very tasty stuffed with Brussels sprouts, they say.) The shock made Labraid lose the power of speech. It even made him change his name to Moen, meaning dumb.

Family friends sent Labraid to Gaul to save his life. He got the power of speech back and used it to chat up a lovely Gaulish princess, then went back to Ireland with an army to take his revenge on the heart-hacking Cobhthatch.

There are two endings to the story:
1 The happy ending – Cobhthatch surrendered but later tried his wicked tricks and had to be chopped.
2 The really happy ending – Cobhthatch and his warriors were trapped in a hall and burned to death.

Either way, Labraid lived happily ever after and all that.

Did you know ...?
The ancient Irish had hospitals. Part of their law (the Brehon Law) said that there should be hospitals for everyone who needed them. The world's first National Health Service? Well, not quite. There were never enough hospitals for *everyone*.

During the Dark Ages Irish medicine and doctors were famous throughout Europe. Dark Age doctors could cut off limbs or even perform brain surgery.

Suffering saints

When the Christian religion came to Ireland, the Irish took to it like a duck takes to water, like the English took to cricket and like Romeo took to Juliet. Monasteries sprang up all over the country like mushrooms and many of the Irish became holier than a fishing net. Some became so holy they were seen as saints.

The Irish Catholics loved their saints. The holy men and women who set an example to the rest. In the Dark Ages (you know, the first millennium or so) a saint was created by a bishop. His people told him there was a wonderful person that they really loved to hear stories about, and the bish said, 'OK! Let's make them a saint!' So popular people and even made-up legends became saints.

If we did that today there'd be hundreds of new saints ...

One saint that was probably just a legend was Saint Uncumber of Flanders. She wanted to be a nun all her life.

So when her father tried to marry her off she simply grew a beard and moustache to put the men off!

OK? Let's make her a saint! (Her dad was crucified as a result but he wasn't made a saint!) Now she's the patron saint of women who want rid of their husbands! But she probably never existed.

Sometimes a dead person would be made a saint because their bones or a bit of their body were said to cure the sick. Dymphna was an Irish Christian girl who ran away from her pagan father. When her father caught her he killed her. No big deal. But when her bones were found they were said to cure people of madness, so she was made a saint.

Bits of saints, 'relics', were worshipped wherever they were kept, and people went around collecting saints' bones! (Don't try this in your local cemetery because grave-robbing is against the law these days.)

Saints still have a place in many people's lives. Many people still wear a medal of St Christopher around their neck to protect them on journeys. And, in Ireland, Saint Patrick still gets you a day off school on 17 March, his feast day.

Saint Patrick *did* exist and he was one of the first people to bring the Christian religion to Ireland. Patrick explained how God exists in three forms – Father, Son and Holy Spirit – by using the shamrock plant which has leaves divided into three parts. He is also said to have driven all the snakes out of Ireland so he has become the patron saint of people who are afraid of snakes. (If you are the sort of person who sees snakes and trembles then either a) pray 'Saint Patrick protect me!' or b) keep out of reptile houses in zoos.) So Saint Patrick's 'emblems' are snakes and shamrock leaves.

What other Irish saints can help you in the 21st century? Here are some suggestions. If you have a problem just say a quick prayer to the right one …

1 Saint Columba

Real or invented? Real person. Born in Garton, Donegal, in 521 and died in 597 at Iona monastery. *Life story:* Went across to Scotland and northern England to convert the people to Christianity. But he may have gone because he'd been a naughty boy in Ireland and started a war that killed 5,000 Irish! *Greatest feats:* He was a great poet and had a voice that could be heard a mile away and killed wild boar with the power of his words – probably shouted a poem at it and burst the beastly boar's brain! He also defeated the Loch Ness Monster with prayers.

Feast day: 9 June

Emblem/relics: 849 relics were taken to Dunkeld in Scotland after he died! Saint of poets … should be saint of people afraid of the Loch Ness Monster!

2 Saint Catald

Real or invented? Probably a real person.

Life story: Toddled off from Lismore Monastery in Ireland to Jerusalem on a pilgrimage. On the way back he was shipwrecked on the south coast of Italy. The people there made him their bishop.

Greatest feats: In return this miracle-man protected the town of Taranto from the plague. This brilliant bish can also protect you against drought, storms, being paralysed, having epilepsy or going blind.

Feast day: 10 May

Emblem/relics: His coffin was found with a carved Irish stick inside. You may like to try a quick prayer if you feel you're going down with the plague:

3 Saint Kevin

Real or invented? Said to have been born around 498. His story may be based on a real person but it was written 400 years after his death (in 618) to attract visitors to Glendalough Abbey.

Life story: An Irish nobleman who gave up the rich life to become a hermit. People flocked to hear him speak and he fed them on salmon – caught by a friendly otter.

Greatest feats: Kevin wanted to be alone to pray. So he went to live up a tree. He still got no peace up there because a blackbird laid an egg in his hand. Old Kev hung on to it until it hatched and the chick flew away. (Which must have been a bit awkward when he wanted to go to the toilet.) A man-eating monster refused to eat kind Kev and in return Kev protected it from hunters. But when a woman (Cathleen) offered to be his charlady and started tidying up his tree, Kev pushed her into a lake where she drowned. He lived to

the age of 120 – so he must have been living in an *elder* tree.
Feast day: 3 June
Emblem/relics: A blackbird. To worship Saint Kevin just climb up a tree and stay there till your 120th birthday, or push an interfering woman into a lake.

4 Saint Brendan

Real or invented? A real person. Lived around 486 to 575.
Life story: A monk who became abbot of the great

monastery at Clonfert. May have travelled to Scotland, Wales and northern France to create new monasteries.
Greatest feats: An angel dropped in to tell Brendan how to rule the monastery and abbots still follow the angel's (and Brendan's) advice to this day. Sailed off with a group of Irish monks and found a happy-ever-after land in the Atlantic Ocean. (Probably not Disneyland.)
Feast day: 16 May
Emblem/relics: Old Bren knew he

was dying. He also knew religious groups would rip his body apart in an attempt to have a relic. So he told a whacking great fib. He said, 'I'm coming back to Clonfert but sending my luggage ahead of me.' In fact his dead body was in that luggage and it was buried secretly before news of the death got out! Sneaky old saint.

5 Saint Brigit

Real or invented? Who knows? Said to have died around 525.

Life story: As a cow-herd child she was baptized by Saint Patrick himself. She went on to become the abbess of Kildare Monastery.

Greatest feats: Lots of miracles. She even changed her bath water into beer – would you fancy drinking it? But she could get stroppy – when Saint Conleth set off to hitch-hike to Rome she was upset and he was eaten by wolves. (Was Brigit to blame?) A fire was burned in her memory for a thousand years ... then spoilsport English soldiers put it out in 1535.

Feast day: 1 February

Emblem/relics: Her image usually has a cow at her feet and her relic is a jewelled brass and silver shoe that can be seen in Dublin Museum. She's the saint of blacksmiths, healers and poets. So say a poem in her honour. Something like ...

A MIGHTY SAINT YOU ARE, GREAT BRIGIT, IN SCHOOL I BET YOU DIDN'T FIDGET

6 Saint Kieran
Real or invented? Probably lived, from about 512 till 545.
Life story: A very holy young man who went to learn about
Christianity from a saint called
Finnian and took a cow along so
he'd always have a supply of
milk.

Greatest feats: Kieran had a tame
fox that carried his homework to
his master. Handy, but don't try it:
when the fox grew big enough it
ate the leather satchel. ('The dog
ate my homework, sir,' has
always been a rotten excuse. 'The
fox ate it,' is even worse.) Kieran
was so good the other Irish saints
were jealous and they all prayed
to God that he would die young. God must have agreed
with them because Kieran died at the age of 33.
Feast day: 9 September
Emblem/relics: Kieran asked to have his body left on a hill-
top so it would be eaten up and leave no bones behind for
pilgrims. But there is a staff in Dublin Museum that might
have belonged to him.

7 Saint Kentigern
Real or invented? Possibly died around 612.
Life story: Kentigern was supposedly born after his mother
was put into a wagon and it was pushed over a cliff into the
sea. (Not likely.) This grandson of a British prince sailed
across to Scotland and converted the Scots in the area we
now call Glasgow. (A bit more likely.)
Greatest feats: A queen came to Kentigern in a panic. Her
jealous husband had thrown her ring into the sea and told
her she had three days to find it … or else. Kentigern told
her that one of his monks had caught a salmon and inside

the salmon was the ring! One early historian reckoned Kentigern died at the age of 185 – probably of old age – but the historian could have been a bad adder and he may have meant 85.

Feast day: 13 January

Emblem/relics: You can still see the ring and the fish on the Glasgow coat of arms. The relics of Saint Kentigern are supposed to be in Glasgow Cathedral today. Go there if you lose your favourite ring and see if Kentigern can help you. You know the sort of thing …

Did you know …?
When Ireland made its own coins in 1926 they planned to replace the English king's head with pictures of Irish saints – till someone said the saints would be upset if they were used for gambling! Instead the new coins had pictures of a salmon, a hare, a cow, a horse and a hen.

The bloody bridal barge

The eleventh century was a dangerous time to live. The Irish noblewoman, Mourne O'Glanny was just setting off to marry the handsome Aran Roe when she got a message from the groom ...

> Darling Mourne,
>
> I've got a bit of a problem, my love. Those villainous O'Flaherty men are out for trouble and they attacked me on my way to our wedding. I'm a little wounded but I'll join you soon. Turn back and wait for me at Sligo Rock.
>
> Aran

Mourne waited a month but it was no-show Roe. Then she woke one night to hear strange sounds and rushed out to see a barge. Aran and his 50 men were chained to the blood-soaked deck of a barge, dead as cow pats and just as covered in flies. She wrapped her Aran Roe in the red wedding cloak she'd made for him and watched over the corpses for a week.

This is all believable. It's the last bit that starts to add a bit of fairy-tale to the history ...

After a week Mourne (who should have been called Mourn-ful) covered the faces of the corpses with gold dust to preserve them. (A bit late there, mate!) Then she set the barge adrift, drank a cup of poisoned wine, and lay down on the barge which her servants set alight.

Naturally, if you go to Sligo Rock, you can still see the ghostly barge with its golden warriors, sailing into the night. Creepy or what?

Super Superstitions

Ireland is the home of the Leprechauns – also known as the Little People ... probably because they're little. A metre and a half at the most.

You'll recognize a leprechaun man because of the feather sticking out of his green cap. These shy creatures are nervous when humans are around so you'll be lucky to see one. But if you do then ...

a) Grab him!

b) Don't take your eyes off him for a second or he'll slip away.

c) Promise to let him go if he hands over his pot of fairy gold.

They all have a pot of fairy gold on their person so don't believe him when he says:

29

Leprechauns aren't the only magic you'll find in Ireland. Here are a few useful ancient spells …

Spelling lesson

Like many ancient people, the early Irish believed in the power of magic forces. You may wish to try these at home, but be warned … If one of these spells turns out wrong, and you end up dead, your money will not be refunded.

1 Make yourself invisible

Let's start with a really fun idea. Make yourself invisible! Walk into class and tweak the teacher's nose. Punch the school bully in the belly, the way you've always wanted to! Get into the cinema free and see those naughty '18' films! Rob as many banks as you can … until you're caught by an invisible police officer and locked in an invisible prison, of course. Here's how …

FIRST YOU'LL NEED YOUR INGREDIENTS. KILL A RAVEN, SPLIT IT OPEN AND RIP OUT ITS HEART. OR POP DOWN TO YOUR LOCAL BLACK-MAGIC SHOP AND BUY A BAG OF FREEZE-DRIED RAVEN HEARTS

TAKE THE RAVEN'S HEART, SPLIT IT OPEN WITH A BLACK-HANDLED KNIFE. BUY ONE IN THE BLACK-MAGIC SHOP WHILE YOU'RE THERE

31

2 Make yourself rich

Have you got penny-pinching parents? A miserly mum and a tight-fisted father? Do they make you slave for your pocket money? Want more money?

Try this Irish magic …

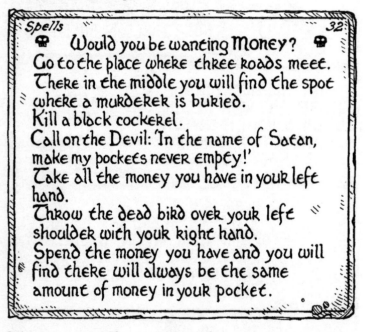

Spells   32

☠   Would you be wanting money?   ☠
Go to the place where three roads meet.
There in the middle you will find the spot
where a murderer is buried.
Kill a black cockerel.
Call on the Devil: 'In the name of Satan,
make my pockets never empty!'
Take all the money you have in your left
hand.
Throw the dead bird over your left
shoulder with your right hand.
Spend the money you have and you will
find there will always be the same
amount of money in your pocket.

3 Avenge yourself on your enemies

Has your head teacher given you a detention just because you painted 'Fat face' on his or her door? Has your next-door neighbour had you grounded just because you used his patio window for a goal in a game of football? Has the local traffic warden fined you for parking your rollerblades on a double yellow line? Has your big sister told your mum who put that frog in the bath?

What you probably want is r-e-v-e-n-g-e ... and r-e-v-e-n-g-e spells 'getting your own back'.

Here's a top twenty of old Irish curses that will have your enemies shaking in their evil shoes ...

1 May the snails devour your corpse and the rains rot it. Worse, may the Devil sweep you away, you hairy creature.

2 May your hens take the foulpest, your cows take the crippen[1] and your calves the white scour.

3 May yourself go stone-blind so that you will not know your wife from a haystack.

4 May the seven terriers of hell sit on your breast and bark at your soul.

1 Never mind what it means. Just say it and when it happens you'll see for yourself what it means!

5 May you suffer hound-wounding, heartache and vultures gouging your eyes.

6 May rain and fire, ill-wind and snow and hard frost follow you.

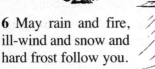

7 I wish you to be tormented with twenty-one demons each tearing you apart.

8 May dysentery[1] take you.

9 May the Devil cut the head off you and make a day's work of your neck.

1 A disease that gives you diarrhoea with lots of blood in the poo! Not only could it kill you – it could make you suffer so much you'll be happy to die!

10 May the Devil swallow you sideways.

11 May the Devil take you by the heels and shake you.

12 May the child within you forever be unborn. Or if he be born, may he not be like a Christian. A pig's snout on him, the mouth of a sheep and the beak of a duck that could dredge the sludge.

13 May you be afflicted with the itch and have no nails to scratch with.

14 The curse of Cromwell[1] on you.

1 Oliver Cromwell (we'll meet him later) was not a popular chap and this is like saying the curse of the Devil on you.

15 May six horse-loads of graveyard clay fall on top of you.

16 The death of kittens on you.

17 My curse on you and ruin to you, you lying thieving rascal.

18 May every day be wet for you.

19 May the cats eat you.

20 May you fall in a nettle patch.

Saint Ruadhan took part in a cursing match with the kings of Tara. Ruadhan cursed the land so thoroughly that Tara was ruined and deserted. Do NOT enter into a cursing match with your teachers. After all, you may just win and end up with a ruined and deserted school. You wouldn't want that, *would* you?

Don't scoff at Irish curses! There may be some truth in them! Look at what happened to King Henry V of England:

- Henry V suffered painful swellings on his bum known as haemorrhoids.
- The patron saint of haemorrhoids is the Irish Saint Fiacre.
- Saint Fiacre had a shrine at Meaux in France.
- Henry's English soldiers wrecked the shrine and Henry believed that brought Fiacre's curse on him.
- It did! Henry's haemorrhoids turned poisonous on 30 August ... which just happens to be Saint Fiacre's feast day!
- He died the next day ... though some spoilsports say he died of dysentery instead.

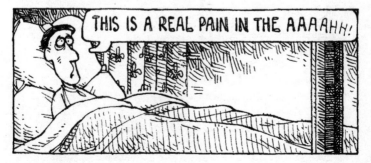

THIS IS A REAL PAIN IN THE AAAAHH!

Did you know …?

Saint Cannera was the patron saint of sailors and he had lived on the island of Scattery. Irish sea captains took pebbles from Scattery Island on board with them. They believed the pebbles would protect them from being shipwrecked.

Killing and curing

If you are sick you go to a doctor. But there were few doctors around in some areas of old Ireland so people learned to cure themselves.

Here are a few cures you may want to try – if you have the brains of a dung beetle …

1 Hangovers

Anyone who feels ill from drinking too much alcohol probably deserves to suffer. Or, in the case of the old Irish cure, deserves to suffer the treatment.

2 Stomach ache

This one would be suitable for the school bully who has a bad belly because he pinched all your sweets and scoffed them.

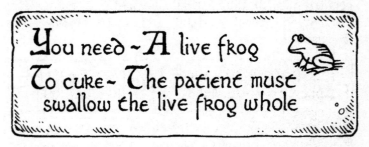

You need – A live frog
To cure – The patient must swallow the live frog whole

3 Warts

Another one of those where you may prefer to suffer rather than take the cure …

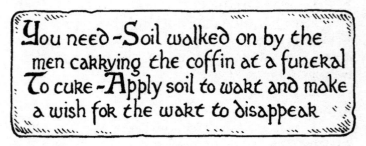

You need – Soil walked on by the men carrying the coffin at a funeral
To cure – Apply soil to wart and make a wish for the wart to disappear

4 Stitch

Ever suffered a stitch – pains in the side – when the teacher makes you run too fast? Here's a simple cure.

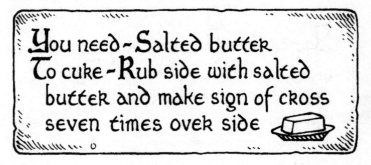

You need – Salted butter
To cure – Rub side with salted butter and make sign of cross seven times over side

5 Water on the brain

There is an old joke that goes:

You would never see such pathetic joke in a *Horrible Histories* book, of course. The old Irish cure was …

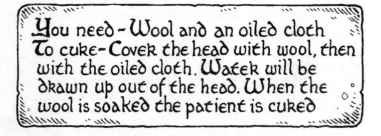

You need - Wool and an oiled cloth To cure - Cover the head with wool, then with the oiled cloth. Water will be drawn up out of the head. When the wool is soaked the patient is cured

6 Mumps

A good old childhood illness that gets you a couple of weeks off school. You get swellings under your jaw and it's painful to swallow. But it could be worse … you could suffer the Irish cure …

You need - A blanket and a pig. To cure - Wrap child in blanket, take to pigsty, rub child's head on back of pig. The mumps will pass from child to pig

Doesn't seem very fair to the poor pig!

7 Toothache
A nice painless way to prevent toothache …

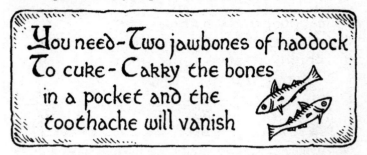

You need – Two jawbones of haddock

To cure – Carry the bones in a pocket and the toothache will vanish

Ever since the miracle of loaves and fishes, these bones have been a magical cure. Unfortunately the fishy bits may start to smell a bit. You will save on dentist visits but you may lose all your friends who think you pong a bit.

8 Lovesickness
Do you want someone special to fall in love with you?

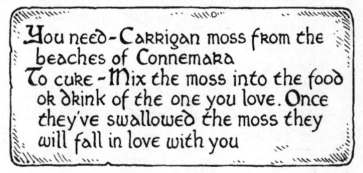

You need – Carrigan moss from the beaches of Connemara

To cure – Mix the moss into the food or drink of the one you love. Once they've swallowed the moss they will fall in love with you

This magical treatment is in great demand all over the world. But the people of Connemara itself don't use the mystic moss for love – they use it to cure their sore throats!

9 Stye
A stye is a painful boil on the eyelid. (If you squeeze it you get an eyeful of gooey yellow pus.) Is there an easier way to get rid of a stye? Yes!

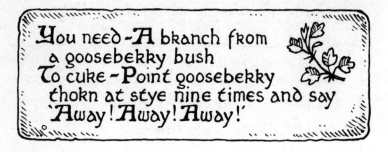

You need – A bkanch fkom
a goosebekky bush
To cuke – Point goosebekky
thokn at stye nine times and say
'Away! Away! Away!'

10 Fever

On Achill Island there is a ruined monastery with a cave
full of old monk bones. If someone in the family is ill with
a fever then the mother of the family must carry out the
cure …

You need – The skull fkom an Achill
Island monk and some boiled milk
To cuke – Pouk the boiled milk into the
skull. Feed the milk fkom the skull to
the sick pekson. (Note: it is veky
impoktant that the mothek should
ketukn the skull to the cave wheke
she found it)

MIDDLE AGES MISERY

In the Middle Ages the people of Ireland were nobbled by the Normans and suffered from the Scots, they were pestered by the plague and finished off by famine. That was Ireland in the measly, miserable Middle Ages.

Miserable Middle Ages timeline

1169 Irish King Dermot loses his throne and, being a bad loser, he invites the Normans across to help him. They help themselves and almost take over Ireland.

1170 Dublin is captured by Norman-English armies and won't be free of English control again till 1922. (That's 752 years if you haven't got a calculator handy.)

1290 Terrible famines drive poor people to the gallows – not to hang themselves but to make a tasty meal from the hanged criminals! Yeuch!

1315–18 Invasion by Edward Bruce and Robert Bruce from Scotland. They think the Irish should join the Scots (and Welsh) to bash the English. They fail, but Scots will be up to their sporrans in northern Irish life for the rest of history.

1336 The English try to ban the Irish language and Irish customs. No chance, lads.

1348 The Black Death kills 14,000. But the English in Ireland complain the plague is killing more of them

than the local Irish! Did the Irish fleas that spread it prefer nibbling English flesh? The Irish desert the countryside for the towns.

1366 A new law, the Statutes of Kilkenny, tries to stop the English who have moved to Ireland becoming too Irish. It says that the English born in Ireland are just as English as English born in England. Their arguments have caused 'hurt and peril' in Ireland.

1400s The English turn the area around Dublin into a sort of fortress called the 'Pale'. The Irish, 'beyond the Pale', were called 'the wild Irish, our enemies' by King Richard II. Just being a 'wild Irish' in England could get you thrown in jail. The English inside the Pale are urged to exterminate the 'wild Irish' outside 'like nettles'. Nice.

1485 The Tudors take over in England with Henry VII. The Irish back a rival 'king', Edward VI, and he's 'crowned' in Dublin. 'Edward VI' is a fake and he fails. Henry VII vows to tame the 'Irish savages'. Not a good start to the Tudor age.

The well taxed family

Your parents probably pay lots of taxes – tax on their car, tax on the money they earn and tax on most of the things they buy. They probably don't enjoy paying taxes, not many people do. So how can they dodge their taxes?

Get them to try this crafty (but cruel) Irish tax dodge. If they save money they might share it with you!

1 FIND A DEEP WELL AND BUILD YOUR DINING ROOM OVER THE TOP OF IT.

2 PLACE A FLOOR OVER THE WELL WITH A TRAPDOOR IN IT.

3 CONNECT A LEVER TO THE TRAPDOOR.

4 PLACE A CHAIR ON THE TRAPDOOR AND ARRANGE THE ROOM SO THIS CHAIR IS AT THE HEAD OF THE TABLE.

5 WHEN THE TAX COLLECTOR ARRIVES INVITE HIM TO DINNER, AND GIVE HIM THE CHAIR OF HONOUR.

6 WHEN HE SITS DOWN PULL THE LEVER AND DUMP HIM IN THE WELL.

This may sound like a fairy tale but it is supposed to be what the O'Flaherty clan of Galway did to the king's tax collectors!

The Normans are coming

William the Conqueror conquered England in 1066 but it was another hundred years before the nasty Normans got around to battering the Irish.

'Strongbow' was the nickname of the Norman Richard, Earl of Pembroke. King Dermott MacMurrough of Leinster invited Strongbow to come to Ireland to sort out his old enemy Rory O'Connor. Naturally Strongbow ended up taking over a large part of Ireland. Never trust a Norman! (The battered Irish believed that King Dermott rotted to death as a punishment for the great sin of bringing over the Normans.)

In 1170 Strongbow's army landed in Waterford. They decided to terrorize the people into giving in. So they didn't simply execute 70 Waterford leaders ... they chopped off their arms, legs and heads and threw the bits off a cliff. Nasty. But not as nasty as the story of Strongbow's son ...

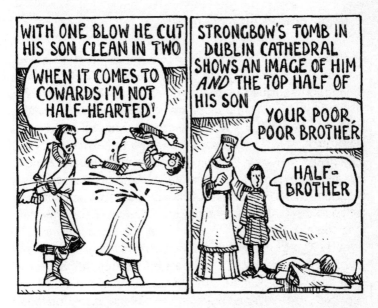

And you thought your dad was mean with your pocket money! At least when he threatens you with a 'cut' he doesn't mean with a sword!

Apart from bringing death and destruction, the Normans brought something else to Ireland. Frogs! Considering the Normans were originally French this was a very suitable thing to bring!

The witch of Kilkenny

There are two sorts of witch. There are the witches in story books who fly around on broomsticks with black cats and may eat children, send princesses to sleep, turn princes into frogs or are just magical friends to sick-making kids.

And then there are 'real' witches. People who were thought to be in partnership with the Devil. Sometimes these 'witches' were asked for simple country charms, cures and curses. Often they were just victims of silly, superstitious people.

In the city of Kilkenny in 1324 a family was accused of witchcraft ... and they had a curious revenge ...

Dame Alice Kyteler was rich. And where there's money there's jealousy. So the cruel gossips of Kilkenny set to work to destroy her.

'Four husbands Dame Alice has had,' Mistress Black said. 'And each one dead.'

'*Strangely* dead, they say! Everyone knows it was murder!' Master Ballyragget told her.

'She should hang for the murders!' the woman hissed.

'But she's too clever to be caught!' the man whispered, and looked over his shoulder as if the Devil himself stood in the shadows. 'They say she uses the black arts!'

Mistress Black hardly dared to speak the word. She just moved her fat lips in the shape, 'Witchcraft!'

Murder was something the gossips couldn't prove so rich Alice lived on with her son, William Outlawe, and her servant Petronella.

But the rumours flew around the city and reached the ears of the bishop himself. He called the gossips before him. 'Dealing with the Devil is a serious charge! A burning matter!' he said. 'So tell me what you have seen!'

The gossips shuffled and looked at one another. Finally Mistress Black spoke up. 'Last Easter I saw Dame Alice sweeping the dust on the road outside her son's house!'

The bishop wrinkled his long nose in disgust. 'Sweeping the road is not against the law of the church! If it was, Kilkenny would have the dirtiest roads in Ireland!'

Mistress Black twisted her fat fingers and her gooseberry-green eyes bulged. 'Aye, Your Grace, but she was muttering a spell as she did it!'

The bishop leaned forward. 'Did you hear the words!'

'I did! But I durst not speak them!'

'Speak them to me, the Lord will understand,' he said.

The woman licked her lips and went on, 'Dame Alice was saying, "May all the wealth of Kilkenny be swept to the door of my son William!"'

'So William Outlawe is in league with the Devil too,' the bishop nodded.

'Aye! And their servant girl, Petronella,' Master Ballyragget insisted. 'I've seen her gathering herbs by the River Nore to put in Dame Alice's cauldron!'

'Aye! It's true!' the other gossips agreed.

And so Dame Alice, William Outlawe and poor Petronella were brought before the bishop and faced with their accusers.

Dame Alice shook her head in disbelief, William shrugged, while poor Petronella just wept.

'I find you guilty!' the bishop roared. 'I sentence you to be taken to City Hall where you will be tied to a stake and a fire lit under you until your godless bodies are burned to ashes!'

Dame Alice looked thoughtful, William frowned and poor Petronella passed out in a dead faint.

But when the next day dawned and the crowds gathered at the City Hall, there was sensational news. 'Dame Alice has escaped!' Mistress Black cried.

'Used her money to bribe her guards, I'll bet,' Master Ballyragget groaned.

'And they say William Outlawe has offered his money to pay for the finest lead roof on our cathedral if only the bishop will spare him!' the woman wailed. 'We've been robbed of our burning!'

'There's still the serving girl,' the man said and pointed down the High Street. The girl was being dragged from the castle while a silent crowd watched with a mixture of hatred and horror.

She was tied with thick rope to the wooden pole that was erected on the cobbles. She was almost lifeless already. Only a soft moaning showed there was still life in her. The black-hooded executioner stepped behind her and, out of mercy, wrapped a cord around her neck and strangled her before he lit the fire. Her moaning stopped.

Someone sobbed in the crowd, someone vomited, but no one left till there was nothing but a pile of stinking ashes on the street and the wind whipped them into the air and towards the cathedral. The stain stayed on the street for many years.

But the story didn't end there. William Outlawe opened his chests of gold and paid for the mighty roof to be placed over the cathedral at Kilkenny.

'It's warm,' Mistress Black smiled as she stepped into the cathedral.

'And water-tight,' Master Ballyragget added.

'And so heavy it is even making those massive rafters sag!' the woman said in awe.

'And crack,' the man said softly, listening to the groaning of the timbers, moaning like a girl condemned to die.

The two gossips couldn't tear their eyes from the dark beam as it began to split and show the pale wood in its heart. When the beam had cracked clean through there was more weight for the others to bear and one by one they snapped with a crack like some hellish whip.

The heavy sheets of lead began to tumble into the church below. The gossips ran towards the altar that stood under the massive church tower. But when the roof fell it pulled down the tower too.

It was over a week before they cleared the rubble and pulled out the twisted corpses.

Of course it could have been just bad luck. It couldn't have been a witch's revenge.

Could it?

Hopeless historians

Historians make mistakes and write them down in books. Then other historians come along, copy the books and copy the mistakes. Even when new historians check the facts people still go on believing the old mistakes! Here are a few historical myths …

Ptick-brained Ptolemy

Take Ptolemy, a Greek who lived in the second century. He said that the Earth was the centre of the universe and the stars were stuck on to a crystal bowl that revolved around us. Wrong, Ptolemy! He also described Ireland …

IT IS FOREVER COVERED BY FOG AND MAN-EATING GIANTS LIVE THERE

Wrong again.

Cracked Cambrensis

In 1188, Norman-Welsh historian Giraldus Cambrensis wrote about Ireland. The Normans had invaded Ireland so cracked Cambrensis had no excuse for his daftness. He said:

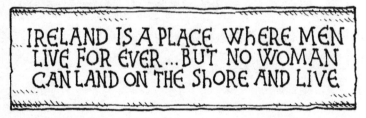

IRELAND IS A PLACE WHERE MEN LIVE FOR EVER … BUT NO WOMAN CAN LAND ON THE SHORE AND LIVE

(Stories like that must have ruined the Irish holiday trade.)

Dopey Donnelly

In the late 1800s an Irish-American 'historian' called Ignatius Donnelly, believed that Irish people had arrived in Ireland as refugees. They had fled from the legendary island of Atlantis when it sank under the Atlantic Ocean.

Dopey? Yes, but even the great British Prime Minister Gladstone was daft enough to believe it! Gladstone backed an expedition to search for Atlantis off the west coast of Ireland.

They didn't find it.

Patrick poppycock

In the Middle Ages there were lots of stories about Saint Patrick. But many of them weren't based on facts. They created three myths about Patrick …

WRONG. The cold and the wet drove the snakes out of Ireland. Roman writer Julius Solanius, writing 200 years before Patrick was born, said, 'In Ireland there are no snakes.'

WRONG. When Roman Britain collapsed some of the new Christians fled to Ireland from the pagan invaders and took their religion with them – years before Patrick.

WRONG. Palladius was appointed by the Pope to be the first Irish bishop. Mind you, he didn't stay long. He couldn't speak the language, didn't like the country and the Irish threw stones at him.

Probably Patrick

BUT, there is a nice story about Patrick that just might be true …

Patrick went to the Rock of Cashel to baptize High King Leary. By then, Patrick was getting a bit old so he always had to stick his bishop's staff into the ground to heave himself on to his feet. Unfortunately the staff went through King Leary's foot and pinned it to the ground. But Leary didn't complain or shout 'Watch me bleeding foot!' because he thought it was all part of the baptism service!

Did you know …?

Patrick may be Ireland's most popular saint, but when he arrived he was NOT so popular with the priests of the old pagan religion … the druids. The druids came up with this nasty poem, attacking Saint Paddy …

Over the sea comes chopper-head,
Crazed-in-the-head,
His cloak has a hole for the head,
His stick is bent in the head.

He will speak unholy words
From a table in front of his house
And all his people will answer:
'Amen! Amen!'

It sounds almost like nonsense … but it's brilliant! You can practically hear them spluttering these words in their rage!

Cross Mac Conglinne

It wasn't only the Druids who made fun of the Christians ... some Christians in the early Middle Ages made fun of themselves! In a book called *The Vision of Mac Conglinne* a monk wrote a story about a hermit who did everything he wasn't supposed to ... and the message was: 'Look at how disgracefully you monks behave these days!' The story went something like this ...

Once upon a time Mac Conglinne was sleeping when he was visited by a phantom that woke him. 'Are you an angel?' Mac asked.

'No I'm a demon from Hell and my name is Dirty-Belch. Now follow me and see how you Christians live!'

So Mac Conglinne and Dirty-Belch set off on a journey in a boat made of beef and sailed through a sea of milk to land on an island made of food.

There they met a hermit. But the hermit was no thin and poor and holy creature, surviving on bread and water! He wore lumps of butter and leeks on his head. 'Look at the books he has to read!' Dirty-Belch sneered.

'Bibles and prayer books and stories of saints?' Mac Conglinne asked.

'Look!' Dirty-Belch ordered.

Mac Conglinne looked and saw the books were made of bacon and sausage and they were the pagan stories of Irish heroes.

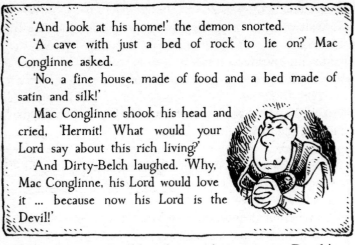

'And look at his home!' the demon snorted.

'A cave with just a bed of rock to lie on?' Mac Conglinne asked.

'No, a fine house, made of food and a bed made of satin and silk!'

Mac Conglinne shook his head and cried, 'Hermit! What would your Lord say about this rich living?'

And Dirty-Belch laughed. 'Why, Mac Conglinne, his Lord would love it ... because now his Lord is the Devil!'

That story was told a thousand years ago. Do things change?

In May 1999 Norman Baker, a Member of Parliament, complained about the luxurious life of British bishops. He said ...

The church should be spreading the gospel, not spreading the fat.

Some things never change, it seems.

Cruel and cwaint cwiz

Pester a parent and see if they can pick out the right answers to this odd and awful Irish quiz ...

1 A 1587 law tried to stop Irish troublemakers disguising themselves and banned the wearing of ...

a) glasses.

b) moustaches.

c) women's clothes.

56

2 Shane O'Neill was an impatient Ulster chieftain. When a servant was late bringing his supper he cut the man's …
a) pay.
b) beer allowance.
c) ears off.

3 In 1525 Abbot Kavanagh wanted to become bishop so he had the old bishop …
a) murdered.
b) locked out of his palace.
c) accused of theft.

4 Some unlucky murderers in Middle Ages Ireland faced a fair trial and an unfair punishment. They had …
a) their skin flayed off.
b) their bowels pulled out.
c) their skin flayed off and then their bowels pulled out.

5 In 1588 many Spanish sailors were shipwrecked off the Antrim coast. The Irish murdered them for …
a) their clothes.
b) their gold.
c) their religion.

6 Aran knitted sweaters are famous for their wonderful patterns. Each family had its own pattern so they could recognize …
a) their father.
b) themselves.
c) their rotten corpses washed ashore from fishing disasters.

7 Neighbours knew when a sick person had died because the family stopped the …
a) milk.
b) clocks in the house.
c) newspaper deliveries.

8 Con O'Neil escaped from Carrickfergus Castle with a rope his wife had hidden in …
a) a cheese.
b) a meat pie.
c) her knickers.

JUST TO MAKE SURE I PUT THE CHEESE IN THE PIE AND THE PIE IN MY KNICKERS!

9 Ireland in the early Middle Ages was divided into two halves – one half were Conn's people and the other half were …
a) Donn's.
b) Mug's.
c) Dugg's.

DONN'S MUG'S DUG!

10 Defenders at Moy Castle tried to protect their walls against cannon-balls. They smeared the walls with …
a) cow milk.
b) cow blood.
c) cow poo.

Answers: 1b); 2c); 3a); 4c); 5a); 6c); 7b); 8a); 9b); 10c).

Talking Irish

The Irish have gathered a lot of wisdom over the years, and have put this knowledge about life into wise sayings – or proverbs – some of which seem a little strange today. But remember, 'Men are like bagpipes, no sound comes from them until they are full.'

Potty proverbs

Here are a few that may help you in your day-to-day struggle with life, parents and school dinners.

1 *A wise woman is better than a foolish doctor.* So, next time you break a leg, run off and find a wise woman. (If she's really wise she'll tell you to hop it.)

2 *While the cat is out, the mouse will dance.*

So, when your parents go out for the night, cancel the babysitter and invite your friends round for a cheese party. (But watch out for traps.)

3 *If you want to be praised, then die; if you want to be blamed, get married.* Unless you are a head teacher, in which case, if you want to be praised fake the school's SATs results! (And if you want to be blamed, get caught.)

4 *It's no use boiling your cabbage twice.* And there's no use washing a body twice. (This is a good excuse if you have had a bath once this year and don't want another one.)

5 *As the old cock crows the young cock learns.* The old cocks being teachers, of course, and the young cocks are the pupils. (But who wants to learn how to crow?)

6 *If you lie down with dogs you'll rise with fleas.*

And you will pick up bad behaviour if you mix with troublemakers. (But a trip to the local pet shop will get you a powder to deal with the fleas.)

7 *It's no use carrying an umbrella if your shoes are leaking.* Good excuse if you skip school on a rainy day to stay in bed. (But remember it's no use carrying an umbrella if your hot-water bottle leaks.)

8 *Don't give cherries to a pig or advice to a fool.* Useful when a teacher is trying to teach you boring history. (It is also useful to remember that you shouldn't give cherries to a fool or advice to a pig.)

9 *One beetle recognizes another.*

And it takes a fool to know a fool. Use this proverb when someone calls you stupid or ugly or smelly. (Of course, it's especially suitable when someone calls you a beetle.)

10 *It's a bad hen that won't scratch herself.* Meaning people should be able to do their own work. Useful when your mother tells you to go to the shop or do the washing up. (But not when your pocket money depends on it.)

Scrambled sayings

Now you've got the idea, you should have no trouble putting the two halves of these Irish proverbs back together. Match the first column with the second. (Work out what they mean – or simply go around saying them, and everyone will think you're brilliant!)

1 A woman's tongue ...	a. speaks the truth
2 Death...	b. is difficult to choose
3 The mouth of the grave...	c. is better than a salmon in the sea
4 A trout in the pot...	d. can lose his hat in a fairy wind
5 Even a tin knocker ...	e. does not rust
6 Between two blind goats it...	f. is the poor man's doctor
7 Any man...	g. will shine on a dirty door
8 When the tongue slips it...	h. gives to the needy one

Answers: 1e); 2f); 3h); 4c); 5g); 6b); 7d); 8a).

And never forget, 'A Tyrone woman will never buy a rabbit without a head for fear it's a cat.'

The Holy holey door

The Irish gave us a phrase that many people still use today. If you take a risk then you are said to 'chance your arm'.

'Where did this curious expression come from?' you ask.

'I'm glad you asked me that,' I reply. 'Because I happen to know the answer!'

In 1492 the Earl of Kildare and the Earl of Ormond had a big row in St Patrick's Cathedral in Dublin. The cowardy-custard Earl of Ormond went off into a room called the Chapter House with his bodyguard and locked himself in.

The Earl of Kildare decided it was a bit of a daft argument and said, 'Come out and kiss and make up.' (Yes, all right, he didn't exactly offer to kiss the Earl of Ormond but you know what I mean.) The Earl of Ormond ignored this offer so the Earl of Kildare used a spearhead to cut a square hole in the door. Then he took a great risk … he stuck his arm through the door and said, 'Let's shake hands!'

That was chancing, or risking, his arm because the Earl of Ormond might well have chopped it off. (No jokes about the Earl of Kildare being a pretty 'armless chap!) But Ormond clasped the hand and shook it. He opened the door and the two men hugged one another.

If you go to St Patrick's Cathedral today you can see the very door with the hole cut out! If you can't get to the cathedral then why not make your own hole using an empty cornflakes packet – stick your hand through, offer it to your deadliest enemy and chance your arm.

Whiskey to keep you frisky

You'll notice that, unlike the Scots and the English, the Irish spell 'whiskey' with an 'e' in it. And the Irish have some words that might seem very strange.

Here are some to baffle your English teacher! Recite this:

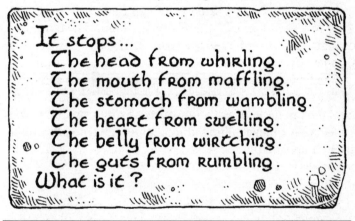

It stops...
The head from whirling.
The mouth from maffling.
The stomach from wambling.
The heart from swelling.
The belly from wirtching.
The guts from rumbling.
What is it?

Answer: Whiskey. So now you know what to do if your dad's belly starts to wirtch!

Did you know ...?
The national drink, Guinness, was in fact an English invention. The porters at London's Covent Garden market drank the dark beer called 'stout' so stout became known as porter. It was brewed by the Guinness family and became Ireland's most popular drink.

Less popular was the 1970s law that stopped people drinking too much and driving. The unpopular minister who came up with the drink-driving laws suffered an unusual revenge. Drinkers put up adverts ...

Can't drink and drive now?
Want a taxi?
Then call Paddy's Taxis. 24-hour service.
Yes! Any time of the day or night.
Special cheap rates after midnight.
Tel: Tipperary 23456

But the phone number belonged to the minister, who was plagued by people calling him all night long, asking him to pick them up from the pub!

Terrible truths

The Irish Gaelic language doesn't have words for 'Yes' and 'No'. So, even when they speak English, the Irish often find another way of agreeing or disagreeing.

An Irish kid might answer like this:

Or:

Torment your teacher with these testing and terrible truths ... or lies. Which are they? Answer 'That's the truth' or 'For sure it's a lie' to these foul facts.

'That's the truth' or 'For sure it's a lie' ...?

1 The Irish fought for the South Africans in the Boer War and captured old British enemy Winston Churchill. (That's the truth.) Because it was near Christmas they let him go.

2 No women were executed for their part in the Easter Rising of 1916. (That's the truth.) But Mary Plunkett *was* executed along with the men who were shot!

3 A troublemaker called Buck English went for a meal in Dublin and shot the waiter dead. (That's the truth.) English got off scot-free.

4 During the Land Troubles of 1820 a landlord, Richard Long, was shot dead in Tipperary. (That's the truth.) His assassins caught him praying in church.

5 *Dracula* was written by Bram Stoker, a theatre manager from Dublin. (That's the truth.) In the book you may notice that Dracula drinks Guinness when he can't get blood.

6 An Irish leader in the Middle Ages had to be a 'complete man' with no bits missing. (That's the truth.) So, to stop a man becoming a chief, his enemies would gouge out his eyes.

7 In 1750 Irish Bishop Rapahoe was shot dead. (That's the truth.) But he deserved it because he was robbing someone at the time.

8 The most famous rebel of the 20th century is probably Che Guevara. But Che could have played football for Ireland.

9 Around 870 John Scotus Eriugena was a strict teacher who forced his students to think. (That's the truth.) His students used their pens to scratch his name in huge letters on the school walls.

10 In ancient Rome, Christians were thrown to the dogs in the arena. (That's the truth.) The Christians were then eaten by natives of Ireland.

Answers:

1 For sure it's a lie. Volunteer O'Reilly admitted ...

> *We had Winston Churchill under lock and key, only it was Christmas time and we'd all of us had a lot to drink and we weren't watching and didn't we let the ****** escape on us.*

2 That's the truth. Because Mary Plunkett was a man! He was a poet and he was christened Joseph Mary Plunkett ... son of George Noble Count Plunkett (curious middle names ran in the family). Plunkett was married the day before he was executed, which must have put a bit of a dampener on the honeymoon.

3 For sure it's a lie. The cost of the waiter was added on to his bill. English was charged an extra £1 and 10 shillings (about £1.50).

4 For sure it's a lie. Richard Long was caught sitting on the toilet. There was no escape.

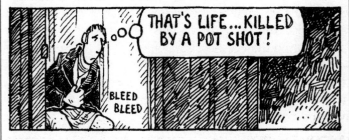

5 For sure it's a lie. Of course Dracula never drank Guinness, but he should have done! Doctors reckon the drink (in reasonable amounts) gives you healthy blood!

6 That's the truth. Of course they could have cut off an ear or a finger to prevent him being a 'complete' man. Ripping his eyes out is going a bit far.

7 That's the truth. The bad bish was a highwayman, a bit like an Irish Dick Turpin.

8 That's the truth. At least in theory – his granny came from Galway so he *could* have represented Ireland at sports.

9 For sure it's a lie. They used their pens to stab the tough teacher to death!

10 That's the truth. Because the dogs that killed and ate the Christians were *Irish* wolfhounds.

TUDOR TERRORS

The Catholics believe the Pope is the head of their Church and more important than the monarch of England. The Protestants protest that the monarch of England is head of their Church and more important than anybody in the world. Both sides will kill (and die) in their thousands as a result of this argument.

Tudor timeline

1520 Henry VIII sends some soldiers to tame the 'wild Irish' – the ones outside the Dublin 'Pale' – but Henry's too busy fighting the Scots and the French and various popes to get very far.

1534 The rebellion of 'Silken' Thomas Fitzgerald against Henry VIII's rule in the Pale. Silk Tom thinks his dad (a prisoner in London) has been executed. Dad's in fact alive and well – 'Silken' Thomas becomes 'Suffering' Thomas when Henry VIII has him executed.

1539 Henry VIII destroys monasteries and Catholic churches, mainly inside the Pale. It doesn't cause too much trouble with Catholics … yet.

1558 Elizabeth I on the English throne. New queen – old problem. The English won't get out of Ireland and haven't the power to crush it entirely. Liz's governor, the Earl of Sussex, says 'I have often wished Ireland could be sunk in the sea.' Charming!

1569 When a rebellion breaks out among the 'wild Irish', the English commander murders innocent farmers. 'If they're dead they can't produce food to feed our enemies!' he says.

1580 Elizabeth is furious when the Irish invite England's greatest enemy, Spain, to land in Ireland. But only 600 land and are captured immediately. The English execute 500 of them in cold blood. Yet …

1588 Spanish survivors of the failed Armada raid are shipwrecked in Ireland. They are mostly massacred … by their friends, the 'wild Irish' peasants!

1594 The Nine Years War starts (and ends nine years later!). Irish chief Hugh O'Neill isn't happy being lorded over by the English – even though they made him 'Earl of Tyrone'. He leads the rebels against English rule.

1598 The north-east area of Ireland, Ulster, now joins in the war and Hugh O'Neill beats the English at Yellow Ford – that's a place in the county of Armagh, not the car he was driving at the time.

1600 The English try a nasty new weapon – famine. They burn the Irish crops and stop the next year's being planted. By 1602 bodies lie in ditches, mouths stained green from trying to eat nettles.

70

1601 O'Neill and those Spanish friends are hammered at the battle of Kinsale. They've really had their chips this time.

1603 Elizabeth pardons the defeated Hugh O'Neill … then she dies. But she's succeeded in wiping out most of Ireland's old chiefs. The line between the 'Pale' and 'wild Ireland' is vanishing. Things will never be the same again.

Horrible Henry's war

No … not Henry VIII, but Sir Henry Sidney, one of Elizabeth's deputies who was sent to rule Ireland. This man wasn't happy with just beating the Irish. He had to terrorize them with a particularly nasty habit he might have borrowed from the old Celts. It was described by another Englishman, Sir Humphrey Gilbert …

> *His order was that the heads of all those which were killed in the day should be cut off. The heads were to be brought to the place where he camped at night and should there be laid on the ground by each side of the path leading into his tent. So that no one could come into his tent without passing through the lane of heads. This brought great terror to the people when they saw the heads of their dead fathers, brothers, children, relatives and friends lying on the ground before their faces.*

The English soldiers copied the evil ways of their leader, Horrible Henry, and fought with far more cruelty than they needed to. One report said …

English soldiers were seen to take up infants on the point of their spears and to whirl them about in their agony. The Catholic Archbishop Hurley had his feet roasted off in a fire in order to make him confess to treason. He was then hanged.
Women were hanged from trees with their children at their breasts, strangled with their mothers' hair.

English troops followed the signals of drummers and pipers while the Irish troops were gathered round a harp player. So the orders went out from England …

Hang all the Harpers, wherever they may be found
By order of
Queen Elizabeth

The English were also pretty good at cheating.

How to win at war by Ivor Trickortoo

The fake friend trick 1

Invite your enemies to dinner. *Disguise your* soldiers *as* servants. *When the enemies sit down to* eat *have them* stabbed to death.

Seventeen Irish leaders died that way. The lesson is, don't accept if the local bully asks you round for tea!

And it's no safer for you to invite him around! Look at the sneaky thing that the English Earl of Essex did to Irish Sir Brian O'Neill …

How to win at war by Ivor Trickortoo

The fake friend trick 2

Accept your enemy's invitation to go to dinner. *Take your* bodyguard. *Enjoy the dinner and wait till your enemy has gone to* bed. Massacre *all the* servants *in the house*. Arrest *the sleeping enemy.*

73

Sir Brian O'Neill and his wife were sent off to Dublin to be executed.

Sick trick

Ulster chief Shane O'Neill was a wanted man, with a reward offered for his head. But when he was murdered, the reward was forgotten and he was buried.

Later an English soldier, Captain Piers, remembered the reward. He had Shane's corpse dug up and the head cut off. It was put in a pot and pickled and sent to Dublin. Piers claimed the reward and was given it! The head was stuck on a pike over Dublin Castle walls.

Cut-throat combat

In 1583 two Irish chieftains decided to settle a quarrel by a fight to the death – mortal combat. This was the last such contest in Ireland and it would have made sensational reading if there had been newspapers in 1583! Just imagine it ...

SCRATCH & WIN! | BINGO | YOUR STARS | BINGO | WIN & SCRATCH!

The Dublin Daily

13 MAY 1583

CONOR CUT TO THE COBBLES

From our ace sports reporter, Sean Short

This morning blood is still being washed from the cobbles of Dublin Castle's courtyard. That's all that remains of the bloodiest combat of the century.

Crowds turned out yesterday to watch two feuding O'Connells settle their differences once and for all. In the red corner was Tadgh and in the blue was Conor. Each man wore just a shirt and a helmet. Each was armed with just a sword and shield.

Before the bitter battle began the furious fighters were searched for hidden weapons – but it's pretty difficult to hide a weapon when you're wearing just a shirt. They sat on small stools in opposite corners of the yard, snarling insults and threatening murderous mutilation to one another. Then the constable of the castle gave the trumpet signal and the two men rushed across the cobbles to do battle.

75

Some spectators were a bit disappointed that the battle was over quite quickly. Terrible Tadgh chopped Conor's legs and cut him twice. The loss of blood soon weakened the woeful warrior and Tadgh was able to snatch his enemy's sword, turn it round and batter at his head with the handle. Conor's helmet crashed on the cobbles and it was curtains.

By this time the crowd were screaming 'Kill! Kill! Kill!' So he killed. Tadgh sliced Conor's head off with his own sword then passed the head to his family.

Today Conor's family were on their knees praying for his soul, while Dublin Castle cleaners were on their knees scrubbing. 'It'll take days to clean this mess up,' Mrs Molly O'Moppet moaned.

Feuding and fighting weren't the only problems for the people of Ireland. There was also hunger and starvation.

What's for dinner?

One of the tales that was told of the 1602 famine was of an old lady who lived near Newry in the north-east. Are you sitting comfortably, children? Then I'll tell you her tale …

Once upon a time there were two poor hungry children who lived on a farm. There was no food for the family and no food for the chickens or cows or sheep or pigs. First the cow died and the little girl cried. But that night the children had cow meat in their soup.

So when the sheep died the little girl didn't cry very much. And when the pig died she didn't cry at all! After a week with no food the children's father died and they buried him in a shallow grave at the edge of the wood.

After another week without food the children's mother

died. 'I'm too weak to bury her,' the boy said.

The girl sighed and said, 'You wouldn't be weak if you had some stew! I'll make you some!'

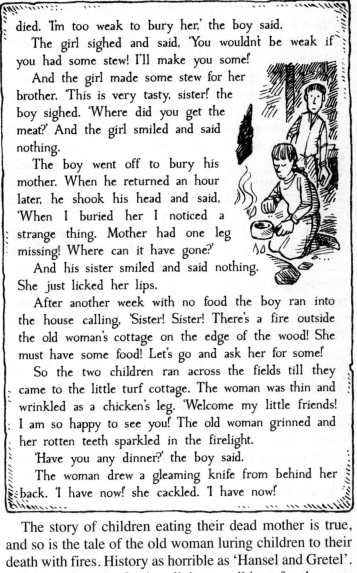

And the girl made some stew for her brother. 'This is very tasty, sister!' the boy sighed. 'Where did you get the meat?' And the girl smiled and said nothing.

The boy went off to bury his mother. When he returned an hour later, he shook his head and said, 'When I buried her I noticed a strange thing. Mother had one leg missing! Where can it have gone?'

And his sister smiled and said nothing. She just licked her lips.

After another week with no food the boy ran into the house calling, 'Sister! Sister! There's a fire outside the old woman's cottage on the edge of the wood! She must have some food! Let's go and ask her for some!'

So the two children ran across the fields till they came to the little turf cottage. The woman was thin and wrinkled as a chicken's leg. 'Welcome my little friends! I am so happy to see you!' The old woman grinned and her rotten teeth sparkled in the firelight.

'Have you any dinner?' the boy said.

The woman drew a gleaming knife from behind her back. 'I have now!' she cackled. 'I have now!'

The story of children eating their dead mother is true, and so is the tale of the old woman luring children to their death with fires. History as horrible as 'Hansel and Gretel'.

Even before the famine, living conditions for the poor were terrible. In 1583, Sir Philip Sydney visited Ulster and spent the night in a peasant's home …

Half a dozen children, almost naked, were sleeping on a little straw with a pig, a dog, a cat, two chickens and a duck. The poor woman spread a mat on a chest, the only piece of furniture in the house, and invited me to lie there. The animals greeted the first ray of the sun with their cries and began to look for something to eat ... I got up very soon for fear of being devoured.

Vile verser

The Tudor poet, Edmund Spenser, took part in the Nine Years War and wrote a very poetic description of the starving rebels of Munster ...

Out of every corner of the valleys they came creeping forth upon their hands and knees, for their legs would not carry them. They looked like Death in human form. They spoke like ghosts crying out of their graves. They ate dead and rotting animals, happy when they could find them. They soon turned to eating one another and did not mind scraping open graves to get at the carcasses. If they found a patch of watercress or shamrocks they flocked around it as if they were at a feast. In the war there were not many who died by the sword, but many who died of famine, which they brought on themselves.

Hang on, Ed! What do you mean, 'which they brought on themselves'?

The putrid poet wasn't saying, 'Look at the sad, starved Irish!' He was saying, 'Look at the Irish getting what they deserved!' You don't need to be a genius to work out that Edmund Spenser was English.

Try a friar

When the Irish went into battle with Queen Elizabeth's English armies they took a few friars along with them. No, NOT 'friers' to make their chips in – 'cos chips hadn't been invented. These *friars* were monks who wandered the land, preaching and being paid by kind people ... kind people who thought that feeding a friar was a good way to get to heaven.

Anyway, friars often joined the Irish armies to pray for the sick (that they would get better), for the living (that they would stay alive long enough to massacre the evil English), and for the dead (that they'd get a nice comfy place with God ... who was on the Irish side, of course.)

Now Elizabeth's English didn't like the Irish very much. But they *really* seemed to hate the friar flying squads who flitted around the fighting. (Really, really, *REALLY*!) In England, Elizabeth's dad had banned monks and got rid of their monasteries. In Ireland, if a friar was captured the English would treat him just a little bit nastily.

Maybe your local priest will let you try some of these torturing Tudor treatments on him.

Flattened friar

FIRST TAKE YOUR FRIAR TO A PRISON CELL - THE DARK, DAMP, DANK, DINGY DUNGEON OF DUBLIN CASTLE WILL DO

LOAD HIS ARMS AND LEGS WITH SO MANY CHAINS HE CAN'T EVEN LIFT HIS HANDS TO FEED HIMSELF

JUST TO TEASE HIM A LITTLE, PLACE A BOWL OF FOOD IN FRONT OF HIM

That's what happened to Father James O'Hea. Just to make it extra nasty he was left for a month with wounds that weren't treated. He later spent more than two years in prison before he was released ... alive!

And Father O'Hea was lucky!

Holy horseman

Friar John O'Daly was captured and he was tied to the back of a pair of horses. Then the horses were frightened and sent charging off down the stony Irish roads. By the time they stopped, the friar's body was torn to ribbons that were scattered over a couple of miles.

Bishop in bits

Conor O'Devany was a Franciscan friar and bishop. In 1612, aged nearly 80 years old, he was accused of treason. His punishment was to be publicly hanged in Dublin, have his intestines drawn out before he was dead and then cut into quarters. The large Catholic crowd felt sorry for him, of course, but they pushed and jostled each other to get scraps of his clothing (or dip cloths in his blood). And they didn't just do this after he was dead – they did it while he was being executed.

Fish friars

Tadhg O'Donnell was tied together with another friar and they were thrown into the sea.

Yo-yo your enemy

Daniel O'Nielan was stripped, had his hands tied behind his back and a rope tied around his body. Dangling Daniel was then dropped several times from a tower and pulled back up again. Finally he was tied head downwards to a mill wheel and used for target practice by English soldiers.

Crushed Catholic

Friar John O'Dowd was captured in 1578. To make him betray his friends a rope was tied around his head and tightened. He didn't talk. The rope was tightened some more until the Friar's eyes burst. He didn't talk. Finally his skull cracked open. He didn't talk … though of course, by then, he couldn't.

Did you know …?
During the war against Queen Elizabeth, the Irish needed lead for bullets, pistols to fire them, swords, daggers and helmets. Where did they get these weapons? Cork? Dublin? France? No. Most were bought from greedy merchants in Manchester, Liverpool and Birmingham.

Awful for animals

Horrible for horses 1

English settlers arrived in Ulster in 1607 and were horrified by Irish farmers who ploughed 'by the tail'.

Four to six horses (or oxen) were fastened to a short plough by their tails. When the hair of their tails was rubbed so short that they could no longer pull, the ploughing stopped.

But horse-lovers needn't worry too much. This sort of ploughing was only done to soft soil. The really heavy ploughing was done with proper harnesses.

The English didn't always speak the same language as the Irish peasants and didn't always understand what they were seeing!

Horrible for horses 2

On 22 June 1921 King George V opened the parliament in Belfast.

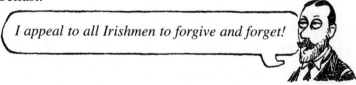

I appeal to all Irishmen to forgive and forget!

The next day the IRA decided to show him how much forgiving and forgetting they planned to do … They blew up the train carrying the king's horse guards.

Four soldiers were killed – but so were *eighty* horses. Of course they were English army horses so they were a fair target ... weren't they?

Horrible for horses 3

Ireland is famous for its horses. So it's not surprising that in 1960 there were demonstrations in Dublin protesting about live horses being sent to be slaughtered for food in France and Belgium. The Irish government agreed that sending horses to Europe to be slaughtered and eaten was not very nice. They decided to stop it ... what happened next?

Answer: The Irish government opened a horse abattoir at Straffan, Kildare so they no longer sent live horses to be killed and eaten – they send dead ones! The horses were saved from sea-sickness, but ended up just as dead.

Cruel for cows 1

Cattle were not popular with poor farmers because they used valuable crop-growing land. The landowners were not popular for putting the cattle there. A cruel but popular punishment was 'tarring and feathering' – the victims had their hair hacked off, were covered in gooey tar and had feathers poured over them that stuck to the tar.

DON'T BE ALARMED DEAR I JUST HAD A WEE RUN-IN WITH SOME LOCAL RUFFIANS

In 1909 the Irish cattle-haters couldn't tar and feather the landowners because many of them lived in England. So what did they do instead?

Answer: They tarred and feathered the cattle that were on their way to market! As they couldn't hack off the hair of the cattle they hacked off their tails instead.

Cruel for cows 2

In the 1920s, when an electric railway opened between Portrush and Ponstewart, local farmers put the carcasses of dead cattle on the line and then claimed compensation for electrocuted cows.

Cruel for cows 3

At the siege of Derry in 1689, the trapped defenders of the town were starving. The attackers allowed some of their cows to graze near the walls. The defenders rushed out hoping to steal a cow or two. They killed 300 attackers ... but failed to capture one cow!

Someone in the hungry town then suggested an experiment on one of the last remaining cows inside Derry. The cow was to be tied to a stake and then burned alive. A sort of steak at the stake. The idea was that her cries would then attract other cows to her rescue!

Fortunately for the cow, it got loose from the flames and escaped.

JUST AS WELL. WE CATTLE ARE NOT USUALLY KNOWN FOR HEROIC STORMING OF FORTIFICATIONS TO SECURE LIBERTY FOR NEAREST AND DEAREST

Dreadful for dogs

You've probably heard the Scottish story of Greyfriars Bobby – the little mutt who stayed at his master's grave and was cared for by the good folk of Edinburgh? Well Ireland has its own faithful hound – but it's an even sadder case!

How can anything be sadder than the little Greyfriars buddy called Bobby? Here's how ...

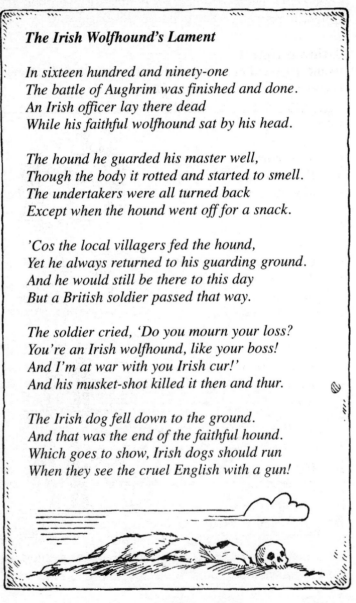

The Irish Wolfhound's Lament

In sixteen hundred and ninety-one
The battle of Aughrim was finished and done.
An Irish officer lay there dead
While his faithful wolfhound sat by his head.

The hound he guarded his master well,
Though the body it rotted and started to smell.
The undertakers were all turned back
Except when the hound went off for a snack.

'Cos the local villagers fed the hound,
Yet he always returned to his guarding ground.
And he would still be there to this day
But a British soldier passed that way.

The soldier cried, 'Do you mourn your loss?
You're an Irish wolfhound, like your boss!
And I'm at war with you Irish cur!'
And his musket-shot killed it then and thur.

The Irish dog fell down to the ground.
And that was the end of the faithful hound.
Which goes to show, Irish dogs should run
When they see the cruel English with a gun!

The dog fell across the bones of his master and they were buried together. Greyfriars Bobby may have been a sad little mutt – but if he'd heard about the Irish wolfhound of Aughrim he would have counted his blessings!

Grimy for geese
Want your chimney sweeping? Can't afford a chimney sweep? Then here's an old Irish way to do it ...

First catch your goose. Hold the goose firmly and attach it to a rope.

Climb onto the roof and drop the goose down the chimney.

The goose will flap its wings and loosen the soot.

Pull the goose back up the chimney.

This is not some Middle Ages madness. The method was still being used in 1955.

SaÒ STUaRT TIMES

After Elizabeth I's armies had battered the Irish their leaders fled. English and Scottish settlers moved into the north-east of the island – they were 'planted' there so the area became known as 'The Ulster Plantation'. The Plantation area was quickly taken over by Protestants.

An early map-maker was one of the first to suffer. The people of Donegal did not want their land mapped and divided up for the English, but they didn't take the map-maker's maps – they simply took his head. The start of another bloody age.

Sad Stuart timeline

1607 'Flight of the earls'. The Irish leaders had been made earls by the English to try to keep them happy. But they were fed-up and went off in a huff to live in Europe. The Irish are now leaderless and the English can control them easily. Hugh O'Neill, Earl of Tyrone, will die homesick and broken-hearted in Rome.

1610 The Plantation starts. At least the 'flight of the earls' is a chance for peace. James I's answer is to take Ulster from the native Irish (who are Catholics) and send in English and Scots (who are Protestants) as farmers. Four hundred years later this is still causing problems.

1616 A hundred castles and 900 great 'English Houses' have by now been built in Ulster. They are defended by thousands of fighting men. Those

Protestants are there to stay.

1641 Fed-up Catholics start the Ulster rebellion. 100 Protestants are thrown off a bridge at Portadown, County Armagh, to drown.

1642 The Protestants fight back. Up to 3,000 Catholics are thrown over cliffs at Islandmagee.

1649 Oliver Cromwell arrives. He calls Ireland, 'That bleeding nation'. He doesn't mess about with revolting Catholics, he exterminates them. He stays just 9 months yet his horrors will be remembered in Ireland for hundreds of years.

1688 King James II is thrown off the English throne, and William of Orange takes it. James is a Catholic and hopes an army of Irish Catholic supporters will help him snatch it back. The Derry Protestants fear this Irish Catholic army has arrived to massacre them. Thirteen apprentice boys pinch the keys to the city and lock the gates. An act that will cause a lot of grief in later years.

1689 The runaway ex-king, James II, now lands in Ireland and is supported by Dublin Catholics. They besiege and starve the Derry Protestants. 'No surrender!' the Protestants cry.

1690 James II, a Scot, supported by the Catholic Irish, loses the Battle of the Boyne to William of Orange, a Dutchman, leading an army of English Protestants.

89

1691 Battle of Aughrim sees 7,000 Irish slaughtered and their general lose his head to a cannon-ball. The Treaty of Limerick puts the Protestants in charge. The Catholics are suppressed. By 1704 they can't vote … or go to school – so it's not all bad news.

Horror stories

As with most Irish history there are so many stories about the 1641 Ulster Rebellion, told by each side, that you could fill more than one book of horror stories with them: in Trinity College Dublin there are 32 volumes of them.

These stories were told in 1641 – but no one can really tell which (if any) are true. You should *not* believe them. But they are *important* because many English people *did* believe them at the time and set out to get revenge.

Here are some of the stories told (and believed) about Protestant sufferings in the Rebellion of 1641 …

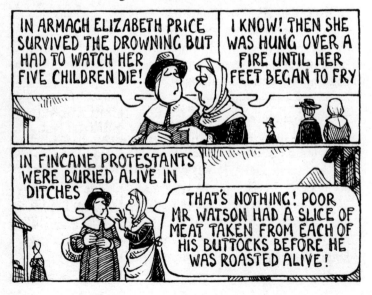

A Protestant historian said that rebels killed 150,000 Protestants in 1641. But that was far more than the entire population! The truth is it was probably nearer 12,000.

And there were other stories that are just as unlikely – ghost stories telling how …

- At Dungannon a huge woman stalked through the town armed with a spear.
- At Lisburn, a phantom battle was fought in the sky.
- At Portadown, a woman – naked to the waist and white with cold – was seen rising from water crying 'Revenge'.

HORRIBLE HISTORIES WARNING:
Never trust a history book!

The reports 'forgot' to mention the stories of what Protestants did to the Catholics.

Then there was the vicious Sir Charles Coote of Cavan. His little joke was to hold the barrel of a pistol to a prisoner's face and say ...

BLOW DOWN THE BARREL PLEASE!

And, when the prisoner blew down the barrel, Coote entertained his troops by pulling the trigger.

Did you know ...?
One of the daftest weapons in history was used at the siege of Ballyally Castle in 1641. It was a cannon ... made of leather. The gun was a metre and a half long, and fastened to a plank which was then dug into a trench. (Don't try this at home with a leather gun made from your grandad's old slippers.)

The gunner put in a cannon-ball and over a kilo of gunpowder, lit the fuse ... and got out of the way sharpish. Just as well. The leather cannon flew backwards and the cannon-ball was still inside it.

READY... AIM... RUN!

The gun was never used again.

Cut-throat Cromwell

It was just a matter of time before the English sent in a large force to get their own back for the rebellion of 1641. Oliver Cromwell, Protector of England, had cut off King Charles I's head and wasn't going to be too bothered about having a few thousand Irish rebels massacred. He arrived in Ireland in 1649.

His visit is still remembered in Ireland as 'Mallacht Cromail' – the curse of Cromwell. What did Cromwell do that was so bad? It's hard to pick the worst but here's a few examples with marks out of ten ...

1 Cromwell was strict with his own troops and had two soldiers hanged for stealing hens from an Irish peasant woman.

2 At Drogheda (north of Dublin) the defenders of a church locked themselves in the steeple. Cromwell's soldiers dragged seats from the church and burned them under the steeple to roast the defenders alive. (One defender jumped and suffered only a broken leg. The English admired his courage and let him live!)

3 Cromwell said of Drogheda, 'I ordered my men not to spare anyone who was carrying a weapon.' This was the usual way of fighting. Cromwell would have said he wasn't to blame when his men killed women, children and priests.

4 Sir Arthur Aston, English Catholic leader of Drogheda's defence, was captured. His wooden leg was ripped off and he was beaten to death with it. Soldiers believed it was full of gold – all they got were splinters.

5 Priests in Wexford were flogged to death then their bodies were flung into drains. Soldiers often dressed in Catholic priests' clothes to make fun of their victims, though it was said that they sickened and died soon after!

6 Cromwell himself led the charge on Mill Mount Tower in Drogheda. The defenders surrendered and expected to be spared. Of course they were all killed.

7 In Wexford 200 women and children were herded into the market place to be slaughtered. Cromwell explained this was a 'righteous judgement' from God ... so that's all right then.

8 In attacking some well-defended places the English soldiers took Irish babies and held them in front as shields.

Just like the tales of 1641 rebellion, there were spooky stories that lived on after Cromwell had gone. They told of ...

- An executioner who killed a priest and was splashed with his blood. The blood could never be washed out of the man's clothing.
- A very holy monk who pulled up the hood of his habit and the English bullets bounced off it.

Ireland hated Cromwell – and Cromwell hated Ireland. He was seasick when he crossed the Irish Sea and never felt well all the time he was there. Maybe that's what made him so vicious.

Kilkenny cats

There's a saying that two people fought 'like Kilkenny cats'. Where does this curious saying come from? (No, the answer isn't 'from Kilkenny' you dummy!) It comes from an old poem that goes ...

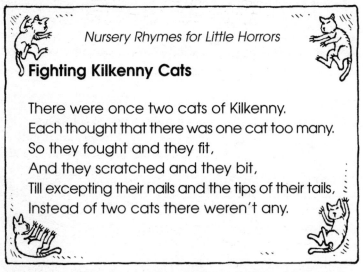

Nursery Rhymes for Little Horrors

Fighting Kilkenny Cats

There were once two cats of Kilkenny.
Each thought that there was one cat too many.
So they fought and they fit,
And they scratched and they bit,
Till excepting their nails and the tips of their tails,
Instead of two cats there weren't any.

But the gruesome question is 'Where did the writer get the idea for the poem?' (Cat lovers skip the following section.)

1 During Cromwell's time a favourite pastime of English soldiers was to tie a rope across the street, then tie two cats together by their tails with a second rope. They would then sling them over the street rope and watch them fight.

fighting like cats and dogs (without the dogs)

2 Cromwell ordered that this cruel game be stopped, but it was still 'played' in secret. One day some of his troopers were fighting cats, when officers appeared. The soldiers had no time to separate the cats, so they just cut them free by hacking off their tails. The cats ran off tail-less.

the cat's away (the mice will play)

3 When an officer asked about the bleeding tails, the soldiers said that the cats had eaten each other except for their tails!

what's been going on? (cat got your tongue?)

The GOOD news is the story is almost certainly absolute NONSENSE! If you want to set two cats free quickly then you just cut the rope in half – you don't cut two tails! (The story was repeated every time some wicked English invaded Ireland – if it wasn't Cromwell's soldiers then it was King George's or somebody else's.)

Did you know …?
What is it about the Irish and cats' tails? An old Irish superstition was that fairies would swap their own babies for human babies. To stop this happening the mothers of new babies could do simple things like:

● Place a prayer-book under baby's pillow.
● Smash a new potato against the hearth.
● Hang up a horseshoe on the doorpost.

But the really nasty way to protect your baby was …

Dim Jim's rebellion

Ollie Cromwell would have turned in his grave! After his death Charles II came to the throne – bad enough! But worse was to follow. Cheerful Charlie's brother, James II, was a secret Catholic who became King of England and Ireland.

James II thought a Catholic army would be more loyal to him, so he gave Richard Talbot ('Lying Dick' Talbot) the job of turning the Protestant Irish army into a Catholic one.

In 1688 Dim Jim lost his throne in England but went to Ireland for help. The new (Protestant) King of England, William of Orange, set about taking Ireland back from Dim Jim and Lying Dick.

Head the ball

Lord Galmoy was annoyed when he was driven off from Crom Castle. All he had were two young prisoners to show for his troubles. He'd make sure they paid for it.

The Catholics lost the war against William of Orange. But the siege of Derry in the north left lasting memories …

Defiant Derry

A Catholic army approached Derry – led from behind by the 76-year-old Earl of Antrim who followed in a luxury coach. It was 7 December 1688.

The Catholic army expected the town to surrender quietly but, when they were just 50 metres from the town gates, a group of 13 Protestant apprentice boys closed the gates and locked them. The siege of Derry had begun.

Since then the apprentice boys of Derry have marched in celebration – you can imagine that, to the Catholics in Derry, this is a bit like waving a red rag in front of a bull! To this day it causes bitterness – some Irish people have 300-year-long memories.

Lying Dick Talbot had massed a large army, and King James himself arrived to command it. It marched under the banner ...

But it is the Protestant cry that is best remembered ...

Although there were some soldiers inside the city whose slogan was …

…soldiers like Commander Lundy who disguised himself and sneaked to safety – his effigy is still burned to this day by some Protestants.

William of Orange finally arrived to help Derry on 28 July 1689 – after the siege had lasted 105 days.

The Catholics were defeated and Dim Jim fled to France. Was he grateful for the way his supporters had suffered in fighting for him? Jim said …

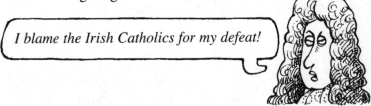

Nice man.

There is a story that Dim Jim fled from the Battle of the Boyne and whinged to an Irish woman, …

Dead dog diet

After six months of being starved in the Derry siege, the governor, George Walker, wrote a 'menu' of the food they had available. This menu has survived ...

horse flesh	1/8d a pound
quarter of a dog	5/6
a dog's head	2/6
a cat	4/6
a rat	1/0
a mouse	6d
candle-tallow	4/0 a pound
salted leather	1/0 a pound
a quart of horse blood	1/0
a horse-pudding	6d
a handful of seaweed	2d
a handful of chickweed	1d
a quart of meal when found	1/0

Notice the quarter-dog is quite expensive. That's because the dogs were fat from feeding on the human corpses!

IT'S A DOG EAT DOG WORLD OUT THERE!

DOG? NO NO NO! I COULDN'T POSSIBLY AFFORD DOG!

Did you know ...?

In 1690, Irish Colonel Richard Grace defended Athlone against King William of Orange. When a messenger called on him to surrender, he drew a pistol from his belt and fired it over the envoy's head, saying:

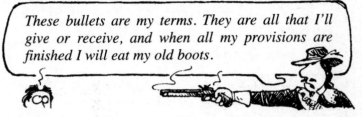

> *These bullets are my terms. They are all that I'll give or receive, and when all my provisions are finished I will eat my old boots.*

Would you eat your boots? Could taste a bit fishy with those soles and 'eels.

Sligo survivor

The Catholics besieged the Protestant forces in Sligo in 1690. If the battle hadn't been so deadly the attack might almost have been funny.

One man must have had an incredible tale to tell. We don't know his name, and he probably couldn't write … but if he could he may have described his incredible but true adventure like this …

> Sligo hospital
> 24 June 1690
>
> Dear Mammy
>   Here I am in hospital, safe and well, so don't worry. But when I tell you the bother I got myself in sure it would turn your old hair grey (if it wasn't grey already, but you know what I mean).
>   It all started when those dreadful Royalist soldiers surrounded this town, trying to take

it for the wicked King James. Of course
we locked the gates and they couldn't get in.
Day and night we marched the walls. They
knew they couldn't get in with ladders, 'cos
we'd have just pushed them down to the
dirty death in the ditch they deserved!
  So they tried a trick so old I think the
Romans used to use it! They built a
wooden tower on wheels and pushed it up
towards the walls.
  Jim turned to me and said, 'That's a
clever idea now, William, isn't it just? Why
didn't I think they'd try that?'
  'Because you're stupid, Jim,' I told him.
  'But it's not clever enough to beat us!' our
captain cried. I swear I never heard him
sneak up behind us and listen to what we
were saying.
  'So how can we stop them, Captain sir?' I
asked.
  'We've been building our own defences and
we have bags full of wood shavings. Go and
fetch twenty bags up here. We'll sprinkle
them with tar, drop them over the wall,

set fire to them and burn their tower to
the ground.'
'Brilliant! Jim cried. 'That's just
brilliant! Why didn't I think of that
William?' he asked me.
'Because you're stupid, Jim,' I told him.
  Now it was a long hard haul up the walls
but in an hour the smarty-pants Royalists
had their tower surrounded by wood
shavings. Then I scratched my head and
turned to the captain. 'How do we set
light to the shavings?' I asked.
'We lower a man down in a basket on the
end of a rope. He sets fire to the shavings
and we haul him back up! Easy!'
  Jim had to laugh. 'I love it. Why didn't
I think of that?' he chuckled.
'Because you've stupid,' I muttered.
'Here's the basket,' the captain said. 'And
here's the rope and a tinder-box. Now just
climb into it, William,' he told me.
  It wasn't until I was in the basket and
being lowered over the walls that I

suddenly thought of something. 'Here!
Why do I have to go?'
'I thought you two loved the idea,' the
captain said and gave orders for me to be
lowered.
Now the Royalists were watching with
interest but didn't quite know what was
going on. When I started sparking the
shavings alight they soon understood
and started firing their muskets at me.
'Get me out of here!' I screamed. Not
that I was scared, Mammy, just they
needed me for my fighting skills at the
top. Royalists couldn't hit a barn if they
were standing inside it. And they didn't
hit me, Mammy. But one lucky shot did
hit the rope and I tumbled back to the
ground. I felt my ankle snap and I may
have given a small cry of pain, but not
much. That's when I thought they would
capture me and skin me alive. There was
no escape, was there? The walls were
high, the gates were locked, even if I
could have crawled around to them.

I could see the enemy move towards me in spite of my friends on the walls firing down at them. Then I saw the most beautiful sight in my life. My friend Jim lowered a second basket down beside me! I scrambled into it and was hauled back up to the top with just a broken ankle and my hair singed off from the blazing tower.

Of course they called me a hero, but it was Jim that made me a live hero and not a dead one. We owe him a lot, Mammy.

I asked him. 'Why didn't I think of a second basket?'

'Because you're stupid, William,' he laughed.

And you know, Mammy, I think he might just be right!

Write soon.

Your loving son,

William

Well? Could you have thought of a way to rescue your friend?

Did you know …?
In the Battle of Aughrim in 1691 the Irish Catholics had French muskets to shoot. They were given English musket balls to pop in the barrel – but English musket balls are too big to fit in the barrels of French muskets!

When the English advanced towards the army at Aughrim the Irish ripped buttons off their uniforms to use as bullets (and it's pretty hard to fight when your trousers are falling down).

The bullets for a musket are pushed down the barrel with a wooden 'ramrod'. These ramrods are a perfect fit for the barrel, so the Irish cut them up and used them instead of bullets. Yes, the Irish tried to stop the English with wooden bullets. They didn't work (apart from giving the odd enemy soldier a nasty splinter). The Irish were massacred.

Wild and Wonderful Women

Women have played their part in the history of Ireland but they're usually forgotten. Women in history often are. So here are a few female facts for you to remember ...

Adamnan's mum

Irish women in the early Middle Ages liked to fight. I don't mean get into a row with the neighbours or smack their husbands round the chops. I mean go into war, battling alongside the men.

That was till Adamnan put a stop to it. Adamnan was the abbot of the important monastery of Iona and when he made rules everybody had to obey him. In the 500s he passed Adamnan's Law which said:

● Women should not fight in armies.
● It is a crime to kill a woman in a war.

Why did Adamnan suddenly come up with this law? Because he was a good lad and he was just doing what his mum told him. She had seen women fighting in a battle, when one female warrior had her breast impaled by a hooked pike held by another woman. Ouch!

> *Adamnan's mum she was the best.*
> *She said, 'Son, you just have to arrest*
> *Any girl, man or wife,*
> *Who picks up a sharp knife*
> *And then sticks it in some lass's chest!'*

Petticoat pirate 1

Grace O'Malley (born around 1530) was the pirate-queen of Connacht (western Ireland) with three galleys and 200 warriors. She cut her hair short and that's probably how she got her nickname – Granuaille, which means 'bald'.

A story says that at the age of 45 she became pregnant, but that didn't stop her pirate attacks. She ordered her ship to attack a Turkish pirate ship. At the height of the battle she went below decks and gave birth to a son. The Turks then boarded her ship and, just as her sailors were about to surrender, she appeared on deck and shot the Turkish captain. (Believe that if you like.)

110

In 1577, she was caught and put into Limerick prison as a pirate. In 1593 she sailed to London to meet Queen Elizabeth I. Grace died in 1603 and is buried in Clare Abbey.

And here's another likely story about her ... Two hundred years after she died, a Scottish farmer sent a ship to western Ireland to loot old cemeteries for bones to grind and use as fertilizer. Unfortunately they pinched Grace's skull and her angry spirit was avenged in a strange way. For one of her teeth found its way into a turnip which the thieving Scottish farmer ate and choked on! (Errr ... how did they know it was Grace's tooth?)

Many ballads were written about gracious but gold-grabbing Grace. This wasn't one of them ...

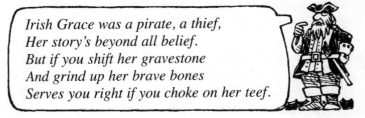

Irish Grace was a pirate, a thief,
Her story's beyond all belief.
But if you shift her gravestone
And grind up her brave bones
Serves you right if you choke on her teef.

Red Mary

Flame-haired Mary Mahon O'Brien lived in Dromoland Castle in 1651 when the English arrived to take it from her. They had killed her husband, Conor O'Brien, in battle and had come to take his castle as their reward.

First Mary told a little white lie ...

CONOR O'BRIEN IS NOT MY HUSBAND AND I AM NOT MARRIED

Well, it was sort of true. Since he was dead he was no longer her husband and she was a widow. But the English

111

weren't going to be cheated out of the castle totally. They said …

FOR YOUR OWN PROTECTION YOU SHOULD BE MARRIED TO ONE OF OUR OFFICERS WHO WILL TAKE OVER THE CASTLE

So red-haired Mary was forced to marry the English soldier, John Cooper. Had Red Mary lost? Not really, because a short while after the wedding John Cooper died. It is said that he fell out of a window … accidentally.

Lady Mary's first husband did die,
So then to another she tied.
He gave her no hassle,
As he fell from her castle,
Bet he wished he had learned how to fly!

Petticoat pirate 2

Anne Bonny came from County Cork and as a young girl lived alone with her father. He didn't want any gossip about him living with a young woman so he dressed her as a boy.

When she fell in love with a penniless young sailor her father threw her out and she sailed off with her lover.

She grew tired of him and went off with a pirate called Calico Jack Rackham, to become the most famous female buccaneer in the Caribbean. She was a great fighter with sword and pistol. With her partner Rackham, she captured many ships.

The pair were finally taken by the British Navy in 1718. Calico Jack had left all the fighting to Anne Bonny and her friend Mary Read. Calico Jack was sentenced to hang, and Anne Bonny was allowed to see him in prison. She told him:

If you had fought like a man, you would not be going to see yourself hanged like a dog.

Then Anne went to trial. A woman witness Dorothy Thomas said ...

The prisoners Anne Bonny and Mary Read were on board the ship that attacked us. They wore men's jackets, trousers and handkerchiefs around their heads. Each of them had a cutlass in one hand and a pistol in the other. They cursed and swore at the men and urged them to murder me so I couldn't give evidence against them in court. I knew they were women from the size of their breasts!

The judge declared the sentence on the women ...

You Mary Read and Anne Bonny are to go from here to the prison where you came from, and from there to the place of execution. There you will both be hanged by the neck till you are dead. And God have mercy on both your souls.

And that's when Mary and Anne played their ace …
They both declared:

YOU CAN'T HANG US! WE'RE PREGNANT AND THE LAW SAYS YOU MUST LET US LIVE!

They were right! Mary Read didn't survive long as she died of a fever in jail. We don't know what happened to Anne Bonny and her child. But let's remember her as an invincible Irish woman …

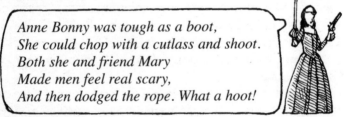

Anne Bonny was tough as a boot,
She could chop with a cutlass and shoot.
Both she and friend Mary
Made men feel real scary,
And then dodged the rope. What a hoot!

The spy girl

In 1920 the Irish Republican Army (IRA) were in conflict with the British. The IRA leader, Michael Collins had a girlfriend called Dilly Dicker. Dilly became his spy on the mail boats that sailed from Dublin to England. She hid in a mail basket to get on board the ship. Dilly climbed out, dressed as a postal sorter and pinched the letters going from Dublin Castle to London. She'd stuff the letters into her underwear and hand them over to IRA agents at the docks.

IF YOU DON'T TAKE YOUR HAND AWAY FROM THOSE LETTERS RIGHT NOW, YOU'LL LOSE IT

She made the return journey and did the same with secret letters from London to Dublin. The IRA knew British plans before the British army in Dublin.

Dilly deserves a poem …

> *An IRA spy, Dilly Dicker,*
> *Was a clever and brave little tricker.*
> *She pinched secret mail*
> *When the mail boat set sail,*
> *And got off with it stuffed in her knickers!*

Of course it is only fitting that these women should be remembered with poems in this style. Because the poems are *limericks* – and Limerick is in the west of Ireland. The origin of the limerick poem is unknown, but it has been suggested that the name comes from the chorus of a 1700s Irish soldiers' song, 'Will You Come Up to Limerick?' Witty people started adding verses of their own in the limerick pattern.

But the limerick is not suitable for a woeful woman like 'Colleen Bawn' … even though her horrible history happened in the county of Limerick.

The 'Colleen Bawn'

To be honest that's not her name, it's a description of her. The words mean lovely girl. She was the most famous Irish girl of the 1800s because a play was written about her. The play *Colleen Bawn* by the Dublin writer Dion Boucicault was hugely popular in Britain and America. It was a 'melodrama', full of sentimental nonsense, dreadful villains and innocent young women. Ever so popular in the days before *Coronation Street* and *EastEnders*.

What audiences loved most of all was that it was based on a true and gruesome Irish murder. Here's a two minute version for you to perform in your drama lesson to a shocked teacher.

115

The Clobbered Colleen

Cast:

The 'Colleen Bawn' 16-year-old Ellen Hanley, a Limerick farmer's lovely daughter.

John Scanlon   Ellen's villainous boyfriend, a posh army officer.

Stephen Sullivan   Scanlon's boatman and partner in crime.

Scene: A boathouse on the edge of the Shannon River.

Music. Enter Scanlon and Sullivan. Loud boos!

Scanlon: It is just a year since I married Ellen, you know!

Sullivan: I know, boss. I was there! I dressed up as a priest and pretended to marry you to her! It was a good trick was that!

Scanlon: But now I am bored with her! I want to go to England and mix with the rich and elegant people. I cannot take a simple peasant girl like Ellen with me!

Sullivan: So what you gonna do, boss?

Scanlon: Tell her that the marriage was a fake! Tell her you were not really a priest. Tell her we are no longer married and that I am leaving her.

Sullivan: She'll not like that, boss.

Scanlon: Then she'll have to lump it.

Sullivan: Ah, but what you did was against the law! If she tells the constable you'll be arrested and go to prison for a long time. They may even transport you to Australia!

Scanlon: Not just me, Sullivan – us! We're in this together.

Sullivan: Oooo-er! I don't want to go to Australia!

Scanlon: Then if she refuses to let me go you will have to kill her! I'll distract her. You smash her over the head with this gun. Row her out into the middle of the river, tie rocks to her feet and dump her. Then we'll be free.

Sullivan: Here she comes now!

Scanlon: Then hide! When I say the word, kill her.

Sullivan: What word?

Scanlon: The words Colleen Bawn!

Sullivan hides. Soft music. Ellen enters

Ellen:	Ah, John, my love. I'm so afraid. Why must we meet in this gloomy place?
Scanlon:	'Tis gloomy news I have to tell you!
Ellen:	Oh, John! I feel a cold hand of fear clutching at my heart. What news?
Scanlon:	The priest that married us was not a priest – he was some vile impostor. We thought that we were married. We were not.
Ellen:	(*Almost swooning in a dead faint, clutches at Scanlon*) Alas, the shame! My father would die of grief if he knew I was living with you and not married! We must find a true priest and marry at once.
Scanlon:	I'm going away to England. We'll marry when I return.
Ellen:	How long my love?
Scanlon:	A year or five!
Ellen:	Five years! I will not let you go!
Scanlon:	Then you must die my Colleen Bawn!

Sullivan steps out from his hiding place. The gun is raised. Dramatic music. Blackout. A scream. A crash. Silence. Curtain falls.

On 6 September 1819 Ellen's body was washed up on the shore of the Shannon estuary near the village of Croom. Scanlon was hunted and found hiding in a hay barn, after a soldier casually prodded a bale of hay with his bayonet.

He was arrested and sent for trial at Limerick. Most people believed that a gentleman would never be convicted of killing a peasant. But he was found guilty and was hanged at Gallows Green in March 1820. There was a story that the horses at first refused to pull his cart to the scaffold, because he was a gentleman!

His boatman, Stephen Sullivan was also hanged. He'd actually murdered the girl – smashing her skull with a gun – after drinking a bottle of whiskey to give himself the courage. But Scanlon died because he gave the order.

Ellen was buried at Burrane churchyard, County Clare.

Woe for women

1 Ulster chieftains looked for brides in Scotland because the Scottish girls brought wedding gifts from their fathers. Not toasters and sets of coffee cups, but axe-men called gallowglasses. When Turlough Lunineach O'Neill married Lady Agnes Campbell of Kintyre in 1568, she brought 10,000 soldiers with her. Irish girls had no chance!

2 Women were sometimes expected to fight in defence of their towns. In 1857 Charles Beggs wrote in his book, *The Military Resources of Ireland* ...

> Cities and towns, if properly defended by the inhabitants, are capable of stopping an organised army. In city fighting every sort of weapon can be used with effect and all the inhabitants, men, women and children, can be usefully employed against the foe. Every brick chimney affords a decent supply of ammunition. A brick, when thrown from the top of a house, provided it hits his noddle, is a certain cure for an enemy soldier's headache.

3 Even in the twentieth century Irish women could be treated like slaves. In 1913 the Irishwomen's Franchise

League told of a girl in a Dublin cinema who was book-keeper, office clerk, cashier, pianist and caretaker – all for 30p per week.

TWO TICKETS FOR THE MATINÉE PLEASE

4 The Irish Republican Army were at war with the Royal Irish Constabulary in 1920. A girl in Newport, Tipperary had her head shaved as a punishment 'for keeping company with a policeman'. Message: Irish girls, pick your boyfriends carefully.

5 In 1888 Jack the Ripper's last victim was Irish girl, Mary Kelly. She went to London to find a better life and instead found a gruesome death. Jack sent her liver to Scotland Yard. Message: Irish girls, pick your men friends VERY carefully.

Burning Bridget

Michael O'Leary was a strange and terrible man. He lived at Clonmel, County Tipperary and in March 1894 he got a terrifying idea into his head. He declared:

MY WIFE BRIDGET IS NOT MY REAL WIFE!

Bridget was 26 years old and a good wife.

Frightened Bridget tried to argue but he became violent. He began to torture her to make her confess. He gathered neighbours and cousins around him to help. He told them …

But the poor woman was too terrified to swallow the food. It was forced down her as she was held down.

O'Leary took the lamp from his table and poured the lamp oil over her. As his neighbours held her down he struck a light and left her to burn to death in the hearth of her house.

121

In time O'Leary and the others were arrested for this horrific crime. But what would you have done with them if you'd been their judge?

a) Find them not guilty and let them go because they had destroyed an evil spirit.

b) Find them guilty of 'manslaughter' – killing by mistake because they really believed the fairy-kidnap idea.

c) Find them guilty of murder and execute them.

Answer: b) The killers were found guilty of manslaughter and O'Leary was sentenced to 20 years' hard labour. But it's scary to think that people could believe in fairies just over a hundred years ago.

GRUESOME GEORGIAN TIMES

In Britain the German Georges were on the throne. The wigs, padded chests and make-up were outrageous – and that was just the men! Dubliners built gorgeous Georgian houses and it became the fine city you can see today. But many Irish people suffered with some new miseries and some old ones ...

Gruesome Georgian timeline

1728 The first of four dreadful famines in the 1700s. The peasants live in poverty while the posh Protestants build Dublin into a grand city as fine as London. This Protestant power is known as the 'Ascendancy' – and of course it makes the peasants jealous and rebellious. Wouldn't you be?

1763 Secret protest groups spring up. The 'Oakboys' object to paying taxes to build roads, the 'Whiteboys' hate the huge rent increases they have to pay for land and the 'Steelboys' in the north struggle against Catholics getting their hands on land. 'Rightboys' in the south-west were often Catholics attacking their own priests. Note: 'Ballboys' collect tennis balls at matches and have nothing whatsoever to do with Irish rebels.

1782 The Irish parliament gets real power for the first time ... for a while.

1798 Wolfe Tone's United Irishmen rise up but are crushed. Apart from getting 30,000 people killed, this gets Ireland's parliament abolished (the English decide it can't be trusted). Ireland will be ruled directly from London for the next century.

Powerful Prots

When James II was defeated the Protestants were in command. They could be generous to their defeated enemies – or they could be cruel. Which do you think they chose? (No prizes for guessing.)

By the end of the 1700s the Protestants were so powerful they could ban Catholics from anything. They even banned them from owning a horse worth more than £5. (The idea was this would stop the Catholics having horses that could be used in a war.) If a Catholic dared to own a horse that was worth more, then any Prot could legally give him £5 and take it.

Seems silly, but according to one famous story it cost a man called Art O'Leary his life. This is how it happened …

- Art O'Leary challenged a Prot to a horse race.
- Art's horse won.
- The Prot then said, 'I'll give you £5 for that horse.'
- Art said, 'No!' and so he broke the law.

- A magistrate (Prot, of course) in the crowd declared, 'Art O'Leary is an outlaw! He can be shot on sight!'
- Art jumped on his horse but was shot down by a soldier.

Most of the victims of this cruel law have been simply forgotten, but Art's story is remembered because his wife, Black Eileen, was a poet who wrote a poem in his memory. The great sadness, for her, was that he died without a priest to say prayers for his soul.

I found you before me dead
Without pope, without bishop,
Without monk, without priest
To say a psalm over you.

Groovy Georgians

Georgian Ireland was as dangerous a time as any other. Sometimes wild and sometimes wacky. Just one of these ten funny facts is false ... which one?

1 Squire Watson of Kilkenny believed that, when he died, he would return as a fox. He had a luxurious marble 'den' built on the grounds of his estate. Daft as a brush! (Fox's tail ... brush ... geddit? Oh, never mind.)

2 Georgian days were the days of bodysnatchers. Doctors wanted interesting and unusual corpses to cut up. Most interesting of all was James Byrne, a 7 foot 2 inch giant. A doctor's servant was set to watch him till he died and be first to grab the body. Poor James is said to have been 'watched to death' when he died of the depression it caused.

3 There was a curious custom in Teltown, County Meath. Couples who wanted to marry simply walked towards each other on Saint Brigit's Day (1 February). If they didn't like one another they could divorce by simply walking away from one another one year and a day later. (This custom went on until the 1920s.)

4 There were so many moles under Cork Cathedral that the floor collapsed during a service and fifty people fell to their deaths. They didn't bother burying them in the graveyard, they simply covered up the bodies with a new floor.

5 The posh Dubliners had a group of party-mad men who called themselves 'The Hellfire Club'. They wanted to know what it would really be like when they got to hell so they set fire to a house and sat inside it drinking! (Not that they'd get a lot to drink in hell, I imagine.)

6 Kit Welsh served for 20 years in the Duke of Marlborough's army from 1692, was badly wounded four times and was decorated for bravery by Queen Anne. Kit

Welsh was a Dublin woman. Her secret wasn't discovered till she retired.

7 The great British general, Wellington, was Irish. He won the battle of Waterloo in 1815 and defeated Napoleon. But he was fighting against a fellow native of Ireland … Napoleon's famous white horse was also Irish! Not a lot of people neigh that.

8 In the 1700s the French were at war with the Austrians. The French hired Irish soldiers to fight for them. The Austrians also hired Irish soldiers to fight for them. So, in the battle of Cremona between the French and the Austrians, who won? The Irish, of course.

9 The Bishop of Derry in the eighteenth century was a nasty, suspicious man. When all his guests had gone to bed he scattered flour on the wooden floors so he could see any footprints. That way he could tell who had gone to whose room during the night! Weird.

10 In 1786 the last wild wolf was killed in Ireland. A hundred years before there had been wolf hunts at Castleknock near Dublin. The prize was £6 per dead wolf – a huge amount in those days. No wonder they were exterminated.

Games you might like to try

Hurling

'Hurling' can mean 'vomiting' and is popular with people who have drunk too much, but the *sport* of hurling is almost as ancient, and still very popular today.

You need
A club (like a fat hockey stick).
A ball (like a hockey ball).

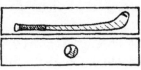

To win
Get the ball into the opponent's goal.
The game is often played between teams from neighbouring villages. But they don't need a playing field – they just play cross-country between the two towns!

Road bowling

You need
An iron ball for each player.
A road.

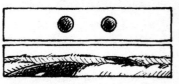

To win
Each player throws their iron ball as far as they can. They pick it up and throw it again … and again … and again … till they reach the end of the road. The player who needs the fewest throws is the winner.

WHERE IS HE GOING?

TO DO SOME MORE HURLING I THINK

Did you know …?

● No one knows quite where the game came from, but there was a law against playing it around the walls of Derry in 1714, so it must have been played in Georgian times.

● The law banned it until the 1950s because people played (and betted on) the game on Sundays.

● The game is still popular in parts of Ireland.

● It's known in Armagh as 'Bullets'.

● The iron ball is about a kilo in weight.

● Danny McParland has an amazing record throw of over 470 metres.

● In Armagh the iron ball is thrown underarm. In Cork they play overarm.

● When they reach a corner the Cork overarm throwers can chuck it across the corner. The Armagh under-armers try to spin the ball round the corner.

● Bullets has its own language – a ditch is a 'sheuth', a 'screw' is a spin and the bowler's assistant who shows the best place to aim is called a 'shower'. The match between two men is the 'score'.

- As it's played on public roads players sometimes have to wait for traffic to pass to take their shots.
- The game is found in Dagenham, England, where the Irish workers at the Ford car factory brought it across.
- Women and children can play too.
- Some historians believe this traditional Irish game came from … England! It may not be wise to say this while watching a game in Ireland.

Foul food

Want to eat like the Irish in the 1700s? Then try this tasty traditional recipe that you won't find in most Irish guidebooks …

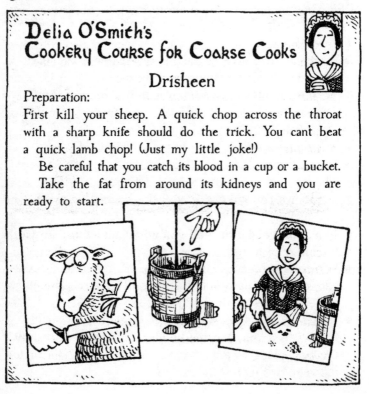

Delia O'Smith's Cookery Course for Coarse Cooks

Drisheen

Preparation:

First kill your sheep. A quick chop across the throat with a sharp knife should do the trick. You can't beat a quick lamb chop! (Just my little joke!)

Be careful that you catch its blood in a cup or a bucket.

Take the fat from around its kidneys and you are ready to start.

Ingredients:
1 cup each of sheep's blood, milk, chopped kidney fat, bread crumbs. And a pinch of salt.

To make:
Put all the ingredients into a bowl and stir them together into a nice thick paste.
Scoop the paste into a pudding cloth and tie it into a ball.
Place the pudding over a pot of boiling water and let the steam cook it for a couple of hours.
Serve it with roast potatoes, mashed potatoes, boiled potatoes, fried potatoes or chips.

Blood-eating sounds pretty gruesome to us but it was common in other countries as well as Ireland.

Of course most meals after the 1600s had potatoes in there somewhere. They even had an old 'Potato Song' to sing.

Pratai ar maidin, pratai um noin,
's da n-eireochainn i
Meadhon oidhche,
Pratai a gheobhainn.

You don't need me to tell you what that means, do you? You can see the Irish word for 'potato' is 'Pratai' – sometimes called 'pratie' in English.

You still can't work out the meaning? Oh, very well ...

Potatoes at morning, potatoes at noon,
And if I were to rise at midnight,
Potatoes I'd get.

And they even had songs of misery about bad potato crops …

Oh the praties they grow small over here,
Oh the praties they grow small over here,
Oh the praties they grow small but we eat them skins
  and all,
Oh the praties they grow small over here.

There aren't a lot of countries where people sing songs about potatoes. It says a lot about the importance of the vegetable in Ireland, although, of course, cabbages and carrots were eaten too.

For flavour they'd throw in some dulse or some sloke. (Seaweed and sea-spinach to you.) Even nettles were used to add flavour to stews.

Steak and kid pie
The Irish writer, Jonathan Swift, lived from 1667 till 1745 and his most famous book is *Gulliver's Travels*. But his most shocking writing was an article he wrote called 'A modest proposal' in which he said …

The Irish peasants are poor and starving because they have too many children to feed and too little land. The English, on the other hand, have plenty of money and are greedy for fresh meat.

The answer is so simple I am amazed that no one has suggested it before. The Irish peasants should sell their children to the English and the English can buy them to eat!

Of course Swift was joking … but a few horrified people believed him. They probably shared a brain with a mashed potato.

Mind you, Swift was a terribly mean man – the sort who may have enjoyed the idea of cheap meat! He used to sit down to dinner opposite a mirror. That way he could see what his servants were doing behind his back. If a butler helped himself to a glass of wine or beer then Swift would take the cost out of the man's wages. That's mean.

Diary of a rebellion

The French had a revolution in the 1790s that got rid of their unpopular king. Some of the Irish decided this was a good idea. A man called Wolfe Tone founded 'The Society of United Irishmen' to start a rebellion. They were mostly Protestants, who hated being bossed by the English as much as the Catholics did. 'The Society of United Irishmen' met in Belfast and had a really good idea …

In 1798 they sent Wolfe Tone to France in disguise, using the code name Citizen Smith, to ask for help ...

The French sent 43 ships with Tone to land at Bantry Bay, Cork ... but the wind drove them back to France. Meanwhile the defenders, mainly Irish Catholics, set about seeking and destroying the United Irishmen. (A lot of Catholics fought against Wolfe Tone's rebellion – they weren't keen on the French, who had been saying nasty things about the Catholic Church since their revolution.)

Flogging was a popular way to make prisoners betray the rebels but, as witnesses said ...

Some stood the torture to the last gasp rather than betray their friends. Others did not, and one single informer in the town was enough to destroy all the United Irishmen in it.

I saw a man being flogged until his flesh was torn to shreds begging to be shot.

Men were flogged until their spines, ribs and livers could be seen.

The rebellion of the United Irishmen broke out in May 1798. The rebels hoped to attack Dublin under the cover of darkness by getting the lamplighters to go on strike, but soldiers with prodding bayonets persuaded the lamplighters to go to work!

In Wexford the rebels, led by a priest, Father John Murphy, had an early success. They defeated men from Cork who pleaded for their lives … in Irish.

At Enniscorthy to the north of Wexford the rebels went on to capture 35 enemy soldiers at Vinegar Hill and shut them in a windmill. The prisoners made a huge mistake. They complained …

The rebels soon sorted that little problem for them …

But by June Vinegar Hill had been taken and Father John Murphy captured. He suffered a brutal execution. (What did you expect?)

In August 1798 Tone and the French finally invaded – too late and too little with just 1,000 men. Wolfe Tone was captured and sentenced to hang. On the morning of his execution he was found to have cut his windpipe with a penknife, but he had failed to cut the artery that would have let him bleed to death. The execution was put off.

After a week in agony, a surgeon told Tone that if he tried to speak it would kill him. Tone replied:

He then died.

But the rebellion wasn't quite over. Some United Irishmen who fled to Paris started it up again in 1803, led by Robert Emmet – another Protestant, by the way. His rebellion was a miserable failure where 80 men turned up to take Dublin Castle with just one ladder. Emmet was hanged, but didn't die a glorious hero. He asked the hangman …

… but he wouldn't drop it! In the end the hangman grew fed up with Emmet saying, 'Not yet!' and he pushed him off …

Chamber of horrors

In waxwork museums the creepiest room is always the 'Chamber of Horrors'. Ireland could have a room all of its own … if you could find a guide brave enough to take you around it …

The resurrection men

Here we have the resurrection men – better known as body-snatchers. There was a great demand for fresh corpses in Scottish medical schools. The Ulster resurrection men dug up bodies from graveyards and shipped the corpses across the Irish Sea in barrels of Irish whiskey to keep them fresh. When the bodies had been removed, they sold the whiskey.

The Burkers

William Burke was born in Cork but made his living in Edinburgh. He started off as a body-snatcher but couldn't be bothered to dig up bodies. He just suffocated victims as they slept in his filthy lodging house and sold their bodies. He was caught and hanged. Suffocating became known as 'Burking'. After his execution in 1830, his skin was made into wallets and snuff pouches.

Billy the Bowl

'Billy the Bowl' terrorized Dublin's streets in the eighteenth century. Billy was born with no legs, so he moved about in

an iron bowl made by a blacksmith, clattering through the cobbled streets. Billy grew tired of begging so, instead, he took to murder and robbery. He was hanged in 1786.

The lynching Lynches

Hanging someone without a trial is known in the USA as 'lynching'. Colonel Lynch, from Galway, moved to America and during their War of Independence he hanged any British redcoats he caught. But he was not as bad as Judge James Lynch. In 1493 he sentenced to death his only son, Walter, for murder. No one could be found to carry out the sentence so Judge Lynch hanged his own son.

The red hand of Ulster

In the Middle Ages a ship carried Scottish chieftains towards Ireland. They agreed that the first chief to lay a hand on the shore would own all of Ulster. Chieftain O'Neill chopped off his own hand and threw it on to the shore. You've got to hand it to him, that was a brave thing to do. To this day the bloody hand is a symbol of Ulster.

cheerless for children

Like children all over the world, Irish children have suffered terribly at times. You had to be tough to survive and sometimes you didn't have a chance …

Cursed kids

Children had their whole lives decided the moment they were born. A candle should be the first thing they saw when they opened their eyes – then they'd grow up to follow good ways not dark and evil ways. The family would examine the baby for moles – they're brown spots on the skin, not the little furry rats that wreck your garden! The position of the mole told you all you wanted to know about the child …

Doctor Spot's Baby Book~

Chapter 13 : Moles

fig I

A mole above the mouth ~the child will grow up to be charming and admired

fig II

A mole under the left ear ~the child will grow up to be hanged

And even a mole-free baby wasn't safe. If a mother wanted to make sure the child didn't grow up to be a thief then she'd bite the child's nails.

Tippling tots

In March 1909 police spies reported that, in one month, 27,999 children had been counted going into just 22 pubs they had been watching. That's an average of forty children every day going into every pub.

Potting pupils

Still, there are worse things than going into pubs – they could have been going to school instead. Schools like Belfast Royal Academy in 1792 ...

BELFAST BOYS BEATEN

The revolution by the boys of Belfast Royal Academy is finally over. Today the boys surrendered to the army who were surrounding the school.

One boy (who wishes to remain nameless) revealed, 'We had heard about the French Revolution and decided it was a good idea.

We plotted to overthrow the staff and take over the school. I suppose we took them by surprise at first. We barricaded them out of the classrooms and taught ourselves – well, to be honest, we didn't do a lot of work!'

Reports have been coming from the school

that there was a plot to assassinate the headmaster. Our inside informant admitted it was true. 'One of the boys had a gun and we planned to shoot him at the first chance we had. Sadly it didn't work.'

The headmaster said today, 'We plan to get back to normal. The staff have agreed to forgive and forget this little problem ... once the disgraceful animals who planned it have been thrashed to within an inch of their miserable little lives! And I'll be first in line with the cane!'

This happy little group of lads probably grew up to be troublesome students. After all they had a good example to follow – the students of Trinity College in Dublin hated Edward Forde, their head or 'Dean'. In 1734 they stoned his windows, so he fired a gun at them. The students ran off – to get *their* guns! When they returned they fired back and shot him dead.

Who'd be a head teacher, eh?

Wailing warnings

The banshee is a charming Irish ghost that warns you when a friend or relative has died. No one quite agrees what a banshee looks like – some are beautiful young women and some are old hags – or even what they sound like – some wail with sickening screams and some are silent. Some are said to be the ghosts of your ancestors. Whatever they are you wouldn't want to meet one on a dark and storm-racked night!

In the 1890s a school reported a curious case ...

9 September

One third form boy, by the name of O'Leary has fallen sick. He finished lunch then complained of pain in the head. He says he can hear someone crying. I listened but heard no one. Still the boy ranted on about hearing this crying, so I sent for the doctor. Doctor Fitzmichael came and he couldn't hear this wailing. He declared the boy had a brain fever and would recover if kept in the dark for two days with nothing but water and beef tea to drink.

11 September

Remarkable and disturbing news came today. O'Leary got a letter from his father to say his older brother has been shot dead. O'Leary read the letter while I was with him. The strange boy just nodded and said, 'So that was it then! The wailing I heard. It was the banshee bringing me the news.' Of course this talk of banshees is nonsense, but I did notice that the brother died just after lunch on 9 September. It does make you wonder.

Lifeless lice

When the Catholics rebelled in 1641 the Protestants were especially keen to murder Catholic children. They believed it prevented the problem of children growing up to be rebels. The nasty little saying among the Protestant soldiers was:

NITS WILL BE LICE!

GULP

In the firing line

In 1922 the Irish Free State was created in the southern part of Ireland. The Protestants in Northern Ireland turned against the Catholics living there. Groups of 'Specials' were formed to help the police sort out the fighting … but the Specials were all Protestants. If Protestants attacked Catholics then whose side would the police and their Specials be on?

Who did the Catholics have to help them? The Irish Republican Army (IRA), who set out to kill police and Specials. War came to the streets and housing estates of the north. Streets where children played. And neither side seemed too bothered about children getting hurt.

February 1922 A bomb was thrown at a group of Catholic children playing in the street. Six were killed.

March 1922 A pub owner and his five sons were taken out of the pub, lined up against a wall and shot.

March 1922 In revenge (surprise, surprise!), the IRA threw bombs into trams and a bomb was thrown into a Protestant worker's house. His two young children were killed.

April 1922 In revenge (surprise, surprise!), the police killed Catholic Joseph Walsh in his bed with a sledgehammer. His 7-year-old son was shot dead beside him.

The IRA started fighting amongst themselves in the south and a sort of peace settled in the north. But the children weren't safe for long. And 76 years later they were still dying.

A bomb in Omagh on Saturday 15 August 1998 resulted in 29 deaths and hundreds of injuries. It was the single worst incident in Northern Ireland during the current troubles. No group claimed responsibility for the bomb but suspicion fell on to a group who call themselves the 'Real' Irish Republican Army.

The bomb caught family groups who were out shopping. Nine children died – 5 girls and 4 boys. The youngest was an 18-month-old baby.

ᾔasτy 19τh cenτury

As the British Empire grew larger and richer, little Ireland was left to get poorer and smaller. (No, the island didn't shrink but the people died or emigrated in their millions.) No wonder it was a century when the Irish hated the British more than ever – if that's possible. Queen Victoria was not popular in Ireland as she was the queen who ruled in Britain while the Irish starved in terrible famines – she was given the nickname 'The Famine Queen'.

Nasty 19th century timeline

1800 'Act of Union'. Ireland's parliament abolishes itself and all the MPs move to London. Not everyone is happy with that idea.

1803 Emmet rebellion against British rule. Less than 100 take part. Emmet is caught and hanged.

1823 Daniel O'Connell founds the Catholic Association and by 1829 Catholics can become MPs.

1845 Potato famine cuts population by over 2 million.

1846 Young Ireland rebellion. Ends with the glorious 'Battle of Widow MacCormack's Cabbage Garden'. Two rebels die and the posh Protestant rebel leader, William Smith O'Brien, is arrested. End of revolt.

1858 Irish Republican Brotherhood (IRB) formed to fight for freedom.

1867 The IRB calling themselves 'Fenians' decide to capture Chester Castle in England, pinch the guns,

pinch a train, drive to Holyhead and pinch a ferry and take the weapons to Ireland. They are betrayed and call off the attack at the last minute. **1879** Protestant Charles Stewart Parnell leads farmers in the 'Land War' when they refuse to obey the landowners and ask for a cut in their rent. The Irish farmers get a better deal but Charlie is a naughty boy. He's been getting too friendly with Kitty O'Shea – the wife of a friend. His supporters turn against him and he dies, just to teach them a lesson. **1893–1912** The British Parliament tries to give Ireland 'Home Rule' – the right to govern itself. Protestants in the north panic and oppose 'Home Rule'. By 1914 they will form a private army – the Ulster Volunteer Force (UVF) – and get guns. So the Catholics in the south will form the Irish Volunteers.

Foul famine

The good news for the poorest peasants in Ireland was that potatoes grew well in their fields. By the 1840s the most popular variety of spud was the 'lumper' or 'horse potato'. It grew on the poorest land and gave a huge crop.

You just planted your potatoes in April and May, picked them in August, then they could be stored and eaten until the following May. During the summer your family had to buy oatmeal to eat until the next crop of spuds – this was the 'summer hunger' but it wasn't too bad. Some potatoes could be fed to your family pigs and they'd give you a bit of meat.

With the help of this super-spud the population rose from 4.5 million in 1800 to 8 million in 1845. That was the good news. But the bad news was that you had no savings because any spare money went to pay your landlord the rent. Still, you survived ... until 1845.

In August 1845 a fungus attacked the potatoes and it spread quickly over the country. The potatoes looked all right, but when you pulled them up they were black and rotten inside, and completely useless.

> *I tried boiling the potatoes in water. The smell was so bad I wouldn't even allow it to be fed to my pigs.*

Lennox Biggar of Dundalk

People went hungry and soon began to starve to death ...

> *I was told of a cabin where in a dark corner lay a family of father, mother and two children lying together. The father was considerably rotted, whilst the mother had died last and had fastened the door so that their bodies would not be seen. Such family scenes were quite common. The cabin was simply pulled down over the corpses as a grave.*

Asanath Nicholson - American visitor

Ms Asanath Nicholson had been in Ireland to give out bibles to the poor (who would rather have had a good meal since most of them couldn't read anyway!). She made one horrific error ...

We crossed to a small island in Donegal in a boat and found it deserted. All we could see were dogs. I wondered, 'How can the dogs look so fat and shining here, where there is no food for the people.' Then the pilot of my boat told me what the dogs were eating.

The misery was recorded by people like William Carleton, who wrote in his book, *The Black Prophet* ...

The roads were literally black with funerals and, as you passed from parish to parish, the death bells were ringing forth in slow and gloomy tones. They were ringing a triumph of Death over the face of our devoted country – a country that was filled with darker desolation and deeper sadness every day.

People would eat anything ...

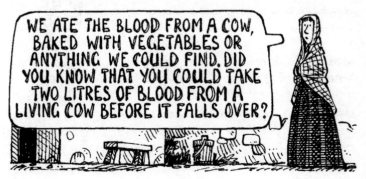

WE ATE THE BLOOD FROM A COW, BAKED WITH VEGETABLES OR ANYTHING WE COULD FIND. DID YOU KNOW THAT YOU COULD TAKE TWO LITRES OF BLOOD FROM A LIVING COW BEFORE IT FALLS OVER?

The countryside was emptied of its wildlife …

> SURE, WE ATE THE DOGS FIRST, THEN THE DONKEYS HORSES, FOXES, BADGERS, HEDGEHOGS AND EVEN FROGS. WE STEWED NETTLES AND DANDELIONS AND COLLECTED ALL THE NUTS AND BERRIES WE COULD FIND. THE PEOPLE ON THE COAST COULD EAT SHELLFISH BUT A LOT OF THEM WERE POISONOUS. MAYBE IT WAS BETTER A QUICK DEATH FROM POISONING THAN A SLOW ONE FROM HUNGER.

When the crop failed again in 1846 gangs of criminals formed known to the police as 'Ribbonmen'.

> MOST OF OUR CRIMES WERE STEALING FOOD AND MONEY. NOW THE PUNISHMENT FOR BEING CAUGHT WAS TO BE SENT TO AUSTRALIA … WHERE YOU'D BE WELL FED! SO IS IT ANY WONDER PEOPLE TURNED TO CRIME? ONE POOR WOMAN WAS CAUGHT STEALING FROM A FIELD. WHEN THE POLICE WENT TO HER HOUSE THEY FOUND A POT BOILING WITH A FEW ROTTEN SPUDS AND A DOG IN IT.

Newspapers reported horror stories…

Recently in Schull, County Cork, two small children wandered into the village crying that their da wouldn't speak to them. Villagers took the children back to their home and found the father dead.

I was sent to look at the grave of Kate Barry. I saw what looked like the tail of a horse lying there. I lifted it and pulled up her skull – the hair was Kate Barry's and her grave had been so shallow the dogs had dug her up and eaten her.

In the coldest winter for years, January 1847, the Government set up soup kitchens to give out cooked food. This was a little better than giving out uncooked food …

Apart from the hunger there was sickness …

TYPHUS, OR BLACK FEVER, WAS SPREAD BY FLEAS. THE DISEASE MADE THE FACE SWELL AND TURN BLACK, THE VICTIMS VOMITED BLOOD AND THEY STANK. WHEN THEY DIED THE FLEAS WOULD FIND NEW LIVING VICTIMS AND SO IT SPREAD. IT BECAME COMMON TO LEAVE A DEAD FAMILY IN THEIR CABIN AND SIMPLY SET FIRE TO IT.

Fever killed ten times as many people as starvation. Sick and hungry peasants couldn't pay their rent. The landlords threw them out! Some fell in the ditches by the side of the roads. Some starving families were taken into workhouses but disease spread even more rapidly there …

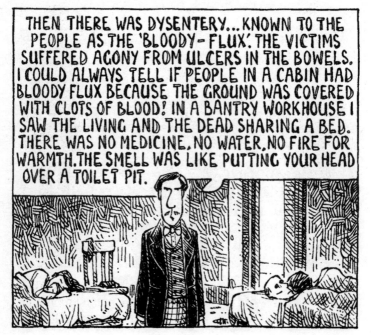

THEN THERE WAS DYSENTERY... KNOWN TO THE PEOPLE AS THE 'BLOODY-FLUX'. THE VICTIMS SUFFERED AGONY FROM ULCERS IN THE BOWELS. I COULD ALWAYS TELL IF PEOPLE IN A CABIN HAD BLOODY FLUX BECAUSE THE GROUND WAS COVERED WITH CLOTS OF BLOOD! IN A BANTRY WORKHOUSE I SAW THE LIVING AND THE DEAD SHARING A BED. THERE WAS NO MEDICINE, NO WATER, NO FIRE FOR WARMTH. THE SMELL WAS LIKE PUTTING YOUR HEAD OVER A TOILET PIT.

Some landlords got rid of their useless peasants by paying their fare on ships to America. But the journey could be a nightmare and many failed to make it. The ships became known as 'Coffin Ships'.

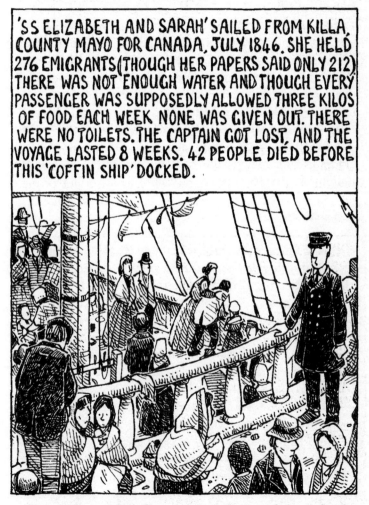

'SS ELIZABETH AND SARAH' SAILED FROM KILLA, COUNTY MAYO FOR CANADA, JULY 1846. SHE HELD 276 EMIGRANTS (THOUGH HER PAPERS SAID ONLY 212) THERE WAS NOT ENOUGH WATER AND THOUGH EVERY PASSENGER WAS SUPPOSEDLY ALLOWED THREE KILOS OF FOOD EACH WEEK NONE WAS GIVEN OUT. THERE WERE NO TOILETS. THE CAPTAIN GOT LOST, AND THE VOYAGE LASTED 8 WEEKS. 42 PEOPLE DIED BEFORE THIS 'COFFIN SHIP' DOCKED.

Sixty ships sank before they even crossed the Atlantic. And, when the Irish arrived, they were often unwelcome in Canada and the USA. They drifted into slums and died in just as much misery. The Irish immigrants also had to suffer US laws which ...

- Taxed them for being Irish (Pennsylvania).
- Barred them from holding official jobs (New Hampshire).
- Banned them from carrying a weapon (New York).
- Made them swear an oath against the Pope (New Hampshire).

There were riots against the Irish in Philadelphia in 1844 where 40 were killed and their church burned down. And they'd left Ireland for a better life!

By 1850 the worst of the famine was over. The potato crop had recovered. But the effects of the famine are still felt in Ireland today. As many as 1.5 million people are thought to have died and 1 million to have emigrated.

Bad British

The suffering of the Irish in the famine was terrible. Some people believe that the way the British government allowed it to happen was even worse!

Even when the British seemed to care they made things worse. A woman called Elizabeth Smith saw one royal visit:

August 1849 – the worst year of the famine. Queen Victoria, Prince Albert and some of her children have decided to visit Ireland for 10 days on a morale-boosting trip. She has grown very fat, is much sun-tanned and too plainly dressed to please the Irish. Yet everywhere crowds of thin ragged people cheered the royal party.

The visit cost £2,000. Enough to feed thousands of starving peasants.

Did you know...?

In 1840 an Irishman, Feargus O'Connor, decided to assassinate Queen Victoria ... but he didn't have a gun. He tried to make one out of a kettle, but it didn't work. Finally he got his hands on a very old pistol. He packed it with gunpowder ... but didn't have any bullets. Feargus stepped out of a crowd and fired the pistol at the Queen as she drove past in her carriage. This pointless action only got him transported to Australia for seven years.

I SHOULD HAVE JUST THROWN THE KETTLE AT HER!

The government had never had to deal with a famine like this before. They did try to help but some of their ideas were pathetically wrong ...

THE BRITISH GOVERNMENT CREATED JOBS FOR THE IRISH TO HELP THEM DURING THE FAMINE. THE IRISH WORKERS, INCLUDING WOMEN AND CHILDREN, WERE GIVEN TASKS LIKE BREAKING STONES. THEN THEY WERE TOLD TO USE THE STONES TO BUILD ROADS. ROADS THAT NO ONE WANTED LEADING TO NOWHERE IN PARTICULAR. IN THE BITTER WINTER OF 1846-7 THESE HALF-STARVED WORKERS WERE WEAKENED BY THE COLD AND DIED. SOME TOWNS REPORTED 100 TO 150 DYING EACH DAY.

The nastiest thing is that some of the British didn't appear to care. The Prime Minister at the time, Lord John Russell, tried to appeal for help from Parliament for the Irish. On March 23 1846 he said ...

> *We have made Ireland the most miserable and degraded country in the world. All the world is crying shame on us but we are cruel in our disgrace and in our failure to govern.*

Parliament generally ignored his appeal.

Some were even vicious in their refusal to help. In Mayo, the worst evicting landlord was Lord Lucan who owned 60,000 acres. He began to 'improve' his land by throwing out starving tenants to make larger more profitable farms. 10,000 peasants were evicted without warning and without compensation and Scottish farmers were brought in to work the new farms. (They were forbidden by Lucan to hire Irish labourers.) Lucan said:

> *They are all Catholics. And I won't breed peasants to pay priests.*

Alfred Tennyson, the famous Victorian poet, thought Lucan was doing the Irish a favour! He said ...

> *The Irish are all furious fools. They live in a horrible island and have no history of their own worth any notice ... Couldn't someone blow up that horrible island with dynamite and carry it off in pieces – a long way off?*

Even government ministers who were supposed to be helping the famine relief said …

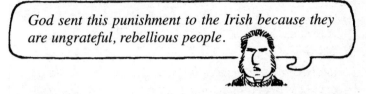

God sent this punishment to the Irish because they are ungrateful, rebellious people.

It is certainly true that the British did not do enough to help. In 1998 Prime Minister Tony Blair went as far as to say 'Sorry' to the Irish for Britain's failure. But there are some lies about the famine that are *still* believed by many people.

Lie number 1:

WHILE THE IRISH STARVED, THE BRITISH WERE SENDING FOOD OUT OF IRELAND TO MAKE MORE MONEY

Not true. Oats, wheat and barley *were* sent out of Ireland – but five times as much food came *into* Ireland to feed the poor. The famine cost the British government £8 million.

Lie number 2:

QUEEN VICTORIA GAVE JUST FIVE MISERABLE POUNDS TO HELP FEED THE POOR

A lie – but widely believed in Ireland until the 1990s. Queen Victoria gave £5,000 of her own money.

Lie number 3:

That wasn't generally true, though some Protestant soup kitchens would only give out food *after* the starving had been to their Bible classes. And some deliberately served meat on a Friday – the day when Catholics were not allowed to eat meat.

Did you know ...?
In Ireland, any patch of white, unhealthy grass is known as 'Hungry Grass' – it is said to be the place where a victim of the famine died. And it is haunted. Don't stand on it! You will start to feel weak, cold and hungry. If you aren't carrying a piece of bread to eat quickly you will die! (It is possible a bag of crisps could save your life but this has never been tested.)

Cattle driving

The Irish farm workers of the 1870s believed the land should belong to them, not to their landlords. The landlords stuck cattle on the land. The farm workers wanted to plough it up and plant crops like potatoes ... but the police wouldn't let them. In 1879 the 'Land War' broke out and this was the game the workers played with the police ...

You need
Cows on a large farm.
Two teams: police and workers.
A plough.

To win
At night the peasants sneak on to the land. They open the gates and drive the cattle on to the road. Next morning, when the cattle are five miles from the farm, the police are called ... 'Some cattle have escaped! Dangerous bulls are roaming the streets!' The police rush to the scene and spend all day trying to round up the cattle, find out where they come from and drive them back.

While the police are doing this the workers plough up the land ... and win! The workers got the right to buy the land they had worked on.

Note: If the landlord is still unwilling to sell then go to his house and dig a grave outside his front door ... a gruesome little message showing what could happen to him!

Wonderful wakes

If you died in Ireland then you would know that your family would give you a good funeral if they possibly could. An Irish send-off is known as a 'wake'. It's not like the English version – a few quick prayers, chuck you in the ground then back to the house for tea and ham sandwiches. No, the Irish tried to do it properly, even in the terrible times of the famine.

A wake would have gone something like this …

Many of these traditions are still kept at some Irish funerals. Rain at the funeral is a good sign, by the way … good for the corpse, that is, but not so good for the mourners who are too drunk to remember their umbrellas!

The Celtic custom

Why would the Irish celebrate somebody dying? Probably because it was an ancient belief left over from Celt days.

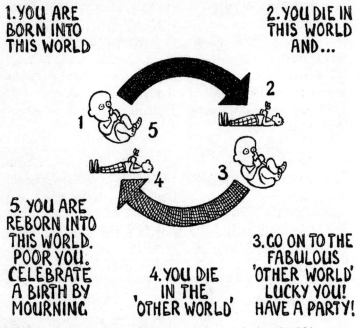

1. YOU ARE BORN INTO THIS WORLD

2. YOU DIE IN THIS WORLD AND...

5. YOU ARE REBORN INTO THIS WORLD. POOR YOU. CELEBRATE A BIRTH BY MOURNING

4. YOU DIE IN THE 'OTHER WORLD'

3. GO ON TO THE FABULOUS 'OTHER WORLD' LUCKY YOU! HAVE A PARTY!

This explained why a Celt was so brave in battle. If he won he was happy – but if he died he could look forward to being even happier! The worst thing was to lose and live. Then he'd have to suffer being sold as a slave. If the Celt warrior's family came to watch the battle, and he knew he was losing, he'd do his family a huge favour ... he'd kill them and then he'd kill himself!

Odd Irish quiz

1 In the 1920s, eleven Irish Republican Army men were captured and threatened with hanging. How did their army chief try to prevent the hanging?
a) He sent gunmen to shoot the judge (so the trial would be abandoned).
b) He sent gunmen to shoot the prisoners (so they couldn't betray their friends).
c) He sent gunmen to shoot the hangman (so there'd be no one to hang them).

2 At the 1789 rebellion at Vinegar Hill, the rebels carried a banner with the letters MWS on. But what did that stand for?
a) 'Murder Without Sin' – in other words this was a holy war where they could kill the English with God's blessing.
b) 'Monster Wexford Stranglers' – to terrify the enemy with their fierce name.
c) 'Mary Washes Shirts' – Mary's laundry sponsored the rebels and in return they agreed to carry her banner as an advert into battle.

3 The Irish writer, James Joyce, wasn't that keen on living in Ireland and went off to Paris with his girlfriend. What was her name?
a) Nora Limpet.
b) Nora Barnacle.
c) Nora Whelk.

4 The 'Royal Dublin Society' erected a huge bronze statue of Queen Victoria opposite the building that became the Irish Parliament. It was taken down. What is there now?
a) A car park for Irish MPs.
b) A toilet for drinkers at the local Guinness factory.
c) The offices of the Queen Victoria Dog Biscuit Shop.

5 Joshua Jacobs was the leader of a nineteenth century religious cult called the White Quakers. Their march through Dublin was a bit unusual and attracted a lot of attention. Why?
a) They walked on their hands.
b) They stamped their heavy boots till the houses quaked (because they were Quakers).
c) They had no clothes on.

6 Irish boys could marry when they were 14 and girls could marry when they were just 12. Of course they can't do that today. When was this law changed?
a) 1772.
b) 1872.
c) 1972.

7 Bishop Walsh of Ossary preached in his cathedral and told the listeners about a man who had run off with another man's wife. The guilty man was in the congregation. What did the man do?

a) Broke down in tears and offered all of his land and money if the bishop would forgive him.

b) Followed the bishop home and stabbed him to death in his house.

c) Ran up to the top of the bell tower and hanged himself on the bell rope.

8 A man called Robert Brooke founded a new village in County Kildare. What happy name did he choose for his village?

a) Successful.
b) Prosperous.
c) Preposterous.

9 Saint Comgall's spit had magical powers. What could it do?

a) Cure the lame.
b) Turn water into beer.
c) Smash rocks.

10 Ireland has an ancient ship-building history. Which unlucky ship was built there?

a) The *Titanic* – famous for sinking.

b) Henry VIII's *Mary Rose* – that sank too!

c) The *Marie Celeste* – found adrift and abandoned in the Atlantic. The crew were never seen again.

Answers:
1c) The IRA men set off to shoot the British hangman, who lived in England. But by the time they got there he had already left for Ireland. The eleven prisoners were spared the rope anyway, so the British hangman went back from Ireland to England while the Irish gunmen went back from England to Ireland. Perhaps they waved as their ships passed in the Irish Sea?

2a) The rebel leader was a priest so the rebels may well have believed that they could Murder Without Sin. Of course they ended up Massacred With Swords.
3b) Nora Barnacle clung to him like a … like a barnacle to a ship's bottom. In the end he married her. You can see Joyce's face on an Irish £10 note because he's an Irish hero. In fact he stuck to his British passport, went to France and refused to return to the country. He also attacked the way the Church ran the lives of the Irish people. So, if you want to be a hero, leave your country with a woman with a name like a winkle and say nasty things about it.
4a) The statue was nicknamed 'The Old Bitch' and it ended up in Australia. Old Vic visited Dublin in 1900 when she was 83. Creepy newspapers said she was given a wonderful welcome … but Dublin papers said an attempt to sing 'God Save the Queen' was a pathetic failure. So don't believe everything you read in newspapers! Another British hero, Admiral Lord Nelson, was even less popular and his monument in Dublin was blown up by the IRA in 1966. Pieces of the

shattered columns went on sale the next day. Someone reckoned there were enough bits sold to make a pillar as big as an Egyptian pyramid. (So watch out for people selling lumps of rock!) It's thought that the hated William of Orange's statue was melted down to plug holes in Dublin's sewers!

5c) If it had been a cold day they'd have been Blue Quakers and if it had been a hot day they'd have been Red Quakers but it must have been in between because they were White Quakers.

6c) So you 14-year-old boys can't pop over to Ireland and marry your 12-year-old girlfriends any longer. Of course you could have done if you were 14 before 1972, but if you were 14 before 1972 you'd be old enough by now to marry her anyway. So save yourself the travel costs and marry her in your home town.

7b) This happened in 1586. The man stabbed the bishop to death. This would never happen today of course, which may explain why fewer people go to church – no excitement like in the good old days.

8b) Brooke went bankrupt (twice), lost his family fortune and died in poverty. Still he asked for it – like someone who calls their football team 'The Unbeatables' or calls their ship 'The Unsinkable'!

9c) Imagine having Saint Comgall on a football team! You know how much spitting those players do! Before half time the pitch would look like the surface of the moon!

10a) The *Titanic* was built in Belfast by the Harland and Wolff shipyard – a Protestant company. Some Catholics reckoned the Protestants stamped 'To hell with the Pope' on every piece of steel. That's why God cursed it and sent an iceberg to sink it. Of course the *Titanic* wasn't all that unlucky. Yes, it *sank*. But only *once*.

TERRIBLE 20th CENTURY

When the twentieth century arrived Dublin was one of the unhealthiest cities in the world. The slums were overcrowded, there were dreadful drains and pathetic poverty.

In the south, the Irish were getting keen on 'Home Rule' to boot out the British. Meanwhile, in Ulster in the north they began to organize themselves to *stop* Home Rule ... at any cost. Ulster people were very attached to Britain and had strong trade links. They also feared that Catholics would interfere in Protestant churches and schools.

The stage was set for a century of violence and misery ... again.

20th century timeline

1914 Ireland is finally granted 'Home Rule' – but the First World War starts, and delays it. Everyone expects it when the war ends in 1918.

1916 The Easter Rising by the Irish Republican Brotherhood, who take over the huge Dublin Post Office and claim Ireland is free of the British. They fail and 15 of them are executed.

1919 Declaration of Independence. The Irish Free State is created in the south but Ulster in the north is not included. Followed by ...

1919–21 Anglo-Irish war. It ends when some rebels agree to a deal with the British government in

169

which King George will still be king of Ireland, and Ulster can stay as part of Britain if the people want (they do). But …

1922–23 … other rebels don't want that and they fight their old allies. A civil war breaks out. The group that wants peace with Britain (the new Free State troops) fight the people who want total independence (the Irish Republican Army – IRA).

1939 Britain fights in the Second World War while Southern Ireland stays out of it.

1949 The Republic of Ireland (or Eire) is created. Trouble is the IRA don't think the republic is complete without Ulster. But the IRA is weak and no one cares too much about what they think. Big mistake.

1967 Northern Ireland Civil Rights Association (NICRA) formed. Mainly Catholics who wanted to protest peacefully for a fair deal over things like voting in elections and housing. The Protestants don't trust the NICRA protesters and …

1968 A NICRA march in Derry is banned. They go ahead anyway and the march is broken up by police with water cannon and truncheons.

1969 The start of modern 'Troubles' in Northern Ireland when Catholics and Protestants riot. The Irish Republican Army supports the Catholics who want to be part of the

Republic of Ireland, while 'Loyalists' fight for the Protestants who want to stay part of Britain. Violence grows as both sides start to use guns. Britain sends in soldiers who at first are popular with many Catholics who see them as fair peace-keepers. But the IRA and Loyalist armies grow stronger.

1971 The first British soldier is killed in Northern Ireland. Sadly there will be another 41 deaths this year, and hundreds more in years to come as the new 'Troubles' get out of hand.

1972 The army loses its image of peace-keeping. Thirteen people are killed on 'Bloody Sunday' in Derry when British soldiers fire at Irish demonstrators. It turns out that none of the demonstrators had weapons. The army is no longer popular, but what will happen if they leave? Will there be even more violence? No government wants to risk it, so they stay … and stay.

1976 Slogans on Belfast's walls include: 'No Pope here!' Underneath someone has written, 'Lucky old Pope!'

1998 Bomb in Omagh kills 29 innocent people.

1999 Politicians continue to talk about peace in Northern Ireland tomorrow. But will 'tomorrow' ever come?

Nasty 1916

By Easter 1916 Irish nationalists wanted freedom from Britain, but Home Rule had been delayed because of the First World War. The nationalists called themselves the 'Irish Volunteers'. A small group of men inside the Volunteers couldn't wait till the end of the war to get that freedom. They planned a violent take-over. The group called themselves the 'Irish Republican Brotherhood' or the IRB.

The workers of Dublin had also formed themselves into a little army of about 250 men, and they called themselves the 'Irish Citizen Army'.

The workers and the IRB marched into Dublin on Easter Monday 1916 and took over the General Post Office in the city centre. The rebels were supplied with guns from Germany – which was at war with Britain at that time.

The revolution was meant to happen all over Ireland but in the end it was only a Dublin rebellion. It was a bit like a fireworks display where only one rocket goes off … and which soon falls back down to earth. They were never going to win, but to some people they became heroes for trying.

So, were the 1916 rebels heroes? Or were they fools and villains? Make up your own mind …

Fools and villains

1 The rebels were cruel. At St Stephen's Green they built a barricade of carts across the road. These carts were pinched from workmen who used them to carry their tools or goods for sale (in the days before white vans). One working man arrived and started to pull his cart out of the barricade. Who can blame him? He was ordered to stop. Warning shots were fired over his head. 'Go and put back that cart or you are a dead man. Go before I count to four. One, two, three, four.' He continued to wheel his cart away. A rifle cracked … and the man sank to the ground with a hole in the top of his head.

2 The rebels could be plain childish. A group from the Post Office tunnelled into a waxworks museum in Henry Street. They made prisoners of war of wax models of King George V, Queen Mary and General Kitchener. The dummies were taken back into the Post Office. Someone put a cigarette case on top of Kitchener's head as a target for ink bottles, thrown by bored young rebels. Later, these figures were put in barricades at the windows. When the Post Office caught alight the wax burned fiercely. You could say their joke backfired.

3 The rebels were badly informed. A rebel group was sent from the Post Office to capture the Telephone Exchange and cut out British messages. Good idea – but they turned back when they were told by an old woman, 'Go back boys, the place is crammed with soldiers.' In truth the building was empty all afternoon.

4 The rebels were just ordinary workers. After the Easter holiday the rebels still held the Post Office. Several rebels asked if they could leave. The leader asked, 'Why?' and they told him, 'Because we'll be late for work!' And normal life did go on during the rising. The St Stephen's Green park keeper, James Kearney, was allowed into the park twice a day to go and feed the ducks.

5 The rebels were often badly armed. One leader, Colonel Plunkett, tried to make a gun from a four-metre drainpipe bound with copper wire and iron chains. To test the gun he stuffed it with gunpowder then scraps of metal, including old razor blades. When it was fired it blew up and almost killed his young daughter. His men then stuck to making two-metre-long pikes with heads from tea caddies and tobacco tins.

6 The rebels were disorganized. They marched up to the main gates of Dublin Castle where a polite, unarmed, middle-aged policeman said, 'Now boys, you shouldn't be here at all.' They shot him in the head. They threw a bomb into the guard house where the guards were eating stew. It didn't explode, but they captured the careless guards anyway. The rebels didn't go on to take the rest of the castle – their first big mistake.

7 The rebels couldn't control the people of Dublin. Mobs went out looting shops. First to go were the windows of Noblett's sweet shop. A crowd of women and children fought over sweets in the street. In Saxone shoe shop, drunken women fought over shoes, only to find that boxes contained only left feet! The writer Sean O'Casey saw a woman use a wrecked tram car as a changing room to try on looted knickers. Mobs flooded in to loot the pubs. It was only when armed rebels went into the street that the mob scattered. After dark, looting began again.

8 The rebels were outnumbered. When they started the fighting the British army had three times as many men as the Irish. By the end of the week they had twenty times as many. To fight against those odds was simply a waste of 450 lives.

9 The British enemy wasn't all bad. In the rising at Richmond Barracks, most of the young rebels were set free. They were told by a British officer, 'You are thoughtless youths … You've been led by madmen. Go home and get your mothers to wipe your noses.'

Or, you could say the rebels were all …

Heroes

1 The rebels usually didn't kill their enemies. When the Volunteers ran into the Post Office, Second Lieutenant Chalmers, of the British Army, was buying stamps. Staff behind counters froze but Chalmers did not see or hear the rebels. The first thing he knew was when a rebel poked him in the backside with a pike. He was taken prisoner.

2 The rebels had a sense of humour. Volunteer Joseph Guilfoyle was sent to guard a railway bridge. Rebel leader Eamon de Valera told him, 'Remember, shoot anything you see in uniform.' Guilfoyle told his friends, 'I just stopped myself from asking if this order included postmen!'

3 The rebels were cruelly killed by better weapons. They dug trenches in St Stephen's Green park. But those trenches were overlooked by the tall Shelbourne Hotel and many rebels were machine-gunned. Private James Fox lost his nerve and ran for the railings at the edge of the park. He was cut down by machine-gun bullets but still crawled on. A second burst killed him. But a British machine-gunner continued to fire at the body. It looked as though Fox was still alive as his body moved under the hammering of bullets.

4 The rebels were very honest. 57 armed rebels set off to Dublin by tram. Volunteer James Brennan held a shotgun in the driver's back while their leader Plunkett paid the conductor for 57 two-penny tickets.

I ASSUME THESE ARE ONE-WAY TICKETS?

5 The rebels included brave women. Rebel women smuggled weapons inside their clothes, and British soldiers were too polite to search them. One officer suggested he could dress up his men as women and *they* could search suspicious Irish women!

EXCUSE ME MISS, WOULD YOU MIND AWFULLY IF I HAD A RUMMAGE AROUND IN YOUR KNICKERS?

6 The British shot innocent people as well as rebels. A blind old man appeared on Eden Quay and as he crossed the road a British sniper shot him. The old man fell writhing to the ground. Henry Olds, of the St John's Ambulance Brigade, ran to help him. He bandaged the wound and helped the man back across O'Connell bridge. The sniper fired twice and both men fell dead. A nun was killed shutting a convent window, and a young girl was killed as she stood in her doorway watching the fighting. One man raised his hand to wave to a friend and was shot dead by a British soldier who thought he was going to throw a bomb. All over central Dublin, the dead were buried in back gardens.

7 The rebels included brave young boys. Rebel captain De Valera tried to send the boys home but many refused. Richard Perle was 16 years old and his mother arrived to take him home. How embarrassing! Children as young as eight played at being rebels – with real rifles they picked up – while their mothers sat on a dead horse and watched. This group marched to the Post Office, saluted, then fired their guns at the building before running off singing, 'We are the Volunteers, And we'll whack the British Army.'

177

8 The British tried dirty tricks. At the Shelbourne Hotel, a British sniper dressed in a maid's uniform and sat at an open window, shooting when he saw a target. At last he was spotted by a rebel sniper and shot dead. In another part of Dublin the British telephoned a shop held by rebels. As rebel Captain MacCormack went to answer the telephone, a friend threw him to the ground ... he guessed a British sniper had a gun aimed at the phone by the window, ready to shoot anyone who answered.

9 The British brutally punished the rebels. The rebels had seized Dublin Post Office and held it for almost a week before they were captured by the British soldiers. That's when the British made the mistake of the century. They sentenced the surviving rebels to death and had most of them shot. The hated Volunteers now became the hero Volunteers! Especially when the people heard horror stories such as the execution of their leader, James Connolly, who was dying from his wounds and had to be propped up on a chair so he could be shot.

Above all it was that last fact that made the failed 1916 rising a curious sort of success. The British were shown to be bullies and even peaceful Irish turned against them. Nobody likes a bully.

Beating the British

After the 1916 rising the British failed to keep their promise of Home Rule for Ireland. So the Irish simply set up their own parliament and ignored the British.

The Volunteers who fought in the 1916 uprising formed themselves into the Irish Republican Army (IRA) and of course violence erupted between the IRA and the Royal Irish Constabulary (RIC). Even though the RIC police force included many Catholics, they were enforcing British rule, so they stood in the way of the IRA.

THE BRITISH SENT IN SOLDIERS IN A BODGED-TOGETHER UNIFORM – ARMY KHAKI AND RIC BLACK BELTS. WE KNICKNAMED THEM THE BLACK AND TANS... THEY WERE HARSHER THAN THE OLD RIC. THEY SHOT SUSPECTED TERRORISTS – WITHOUT TRIAL AND SOMETIMES WITHOUT EVEN QUESTIONING THEM – THEY BURNED BUILDINGS IN REVENGE ATTACKS AND MACHINE-GUNNED INNOCENT PEOPLE AT A FOOTBALL MATCH. MOST OF THE PEOPLE IN THE SOUTH SUPPORTED US. WE WERE JUST ORDINARY MEN WHOSE JOB WAS TO MAKE THE BRITISH GO HOME... ANY WAY WE COULD

THE IRA FOUGHT A GUERRILLA WAR – NO UNIFORMS. THEY FOUGHT LIKE COWARDS WITH AMBUSHES AND MURDERS – THEY KILLED OFFICERS IN THEIR HOMES IN FRONT OF THEIR WIVES AND CHILDREN. THEY EVEN EXECUTED THEIR OWN PEOPLE WHO 'INFORMED' ON THEM. THERE WAS NEVER OPEN WARFARE THE WAY WE LIKED TO FIGHT! MOST OF THE PEOPLE IN THE NORTH SUPPORTED US. WE WERE JUST ORDINARY MEN WHOSE JOB WAS TO FIND THE IRA MEMBERS AND STOP THEM... ANY WAY WE COULD

Like a football match with two opposite goals – but no rules and some ruthless, dirty players on both sides. A lot of people would get hurt. The British refused to call it a 'War' so it became known as the 'Troubles'.

Some odd things happened in the Troubles of 1919–21 …

- Catholic priests sometimes excused IRA killers. One said, 'If you think you did right shooting that man then you are forgiven – and carry on with the good work!'

- Black and Tans sometimes worked in plain clothes to catch the IRA enemy. But in Limerick they were shot at by their RIC friends and in the gun battle three were killed. They didn't need the IRA to kill them!

- In West Mayo the IRA set up an ambush for the RIC. They had to wait in hiding all day … and fell asleep! The RIC spotted them, killed five of them and arrested the other six.

- An RIC constable went up to a local IRA man at Monastervin and asked, 'Are you planning to attack our station tonight? 'Cos if you are I could just take the night off!'

- Miss Winifred Barrington was driving through County Tipperary with Major Biggs, an RIC inspector, when their car was ambushed by the IRA. She was wearing Major Biggs' police cap. Gunmen shot her by mistake.

- The IRA struggled to supply ammunition to their fighting men. By the end of the fighting the men of West Mayo ran out of bullets in an ambush and ended up throwing stones.

• In Dublin RIC patrols were attacked with something worse than stones. Householders emptied toilet pots over their heads!

The IRA may not have dressed like soldiers but they made out reports in a military way. They make chilling reading like this one from Dublin ...

April 1921

We saw a man who aroused our suspicions ... We held him up and searched him and found an ex-soldiers badge in his pocket. We demanded a confession which he refused to give. We then took off his belt, put it round his neck and proceeded to strangle him. Not till he was blue in the face did he admit that he was a Black and Tan on weekend leave ... I put my revolver to his head and asked him to give us information or say his prayers. He refused to tell us anything ... I had no alternative but to fire. He fell and I leant over him and put another round into him.

The dirtiest wars

In 1921 the British decided to divide Ireland into two. In the end, the Protestants in the six counties of Ulster to the north (with a lot of unhappy Catholics) stayed British, while the Catholics in the south (with a lot of unhappy Protestants) became the Irish Free State.

The British Prime Minister, Lloyd George, decided on the border and the southern Irish didn't get much say in where the border should be. He *tried* to make everyone happy, but he hardly made anyone happy.

In the south the IRA didn't like the new arrangement so they fought against their own new government. The new Irish Free State Army had been rebels fighting against the British in 1921. Now they were fighting against their old friends, the Irish Republican Army. And the nastiest wars in history are often the ones where old friends fall out.

The Kerry rope trick

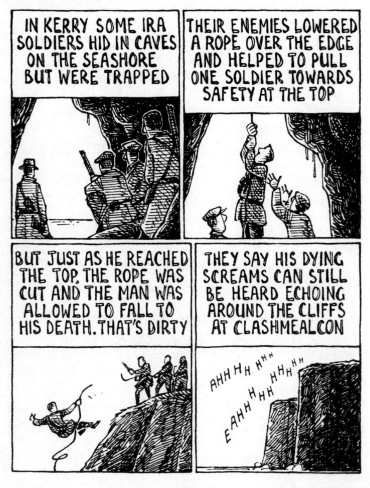

IN KERRY SOME IRA SOLDIERS HID IN CAVES ON THE SEASHORE BUT WERE TRAPPED

THEIR ENEMIES LOWERED A ROPE OVER THE EDGE AND HELPED TO PULL ONE SOLDIER TOWARDS SAFETY AT THE TOP

BUT JUST AS HE REACHED THE TOP, THE ROPE WAS CUT AND THE MAN WAS ALLOWED TO FALL TO HIS DEATH. THAT'S DIRTY

THEY SAY HIS DYING SCREAMS CAN STILL BE HEARD ECHOING AROUND THE CLIFFS AT CLASHMEALCON

AHHHHHHHH
EAHHHHHHHHHH

The Ballyseedy blast

1 IRA soldiers had built barricades to block roads and laid 'mines' – bombs that would be set off by anyone who tried to get past them.

2 When the Free State soldiers arrived at the barricades they took IRA prisoners and forced them to walk into the barricades. At Ballyseedy nine men were tied together and sent to their deaths. Of course the IRA prisoners had not been tried or found guilty of anything. That's dirty.

3 Amazingly one man was blown clear across a hedge into a field and survived.

4 Nine coffins had been prepared so nine coffins went to the funeral. The mourners tore open the coffins to try to find out who was dead and who had survived. Gruesome.

An IRA soldier was executed by the Free State. As he wrote in his final letter …

> 25 April 1923
>
> I have been in the IRA since 1916 and I fought the British. It is very hard to know that it is my own countrymen who are putting me to death

Says it all really.

Poisonous policemen

After 1921, while the civil war was being fought in the south, the Catholics of Ulster were being attacked by the Protestants. You'd have thought the Ulster police would have protected them, but in fact the Ulster police could be just as brutal to the Catholics.

One Head Constable used a bayonet to stab his victims to death because it was slower and more painful than shooting them. And a group of eight policemen got away with murder ... *really* got away with murder. Even though they made the most amazing mistake ...

The eight policemen went to the home of the Duffin brothers and shot them using silencers on their guns so they wouldn't be heard. They left the scene of the murders without being seen, but they carelessly left a clue behind. It was the station police dog! It had followed them to the Duffin house and had been accidentally left inside by the murderers. Next morning, in full view of the whole street, one of the policemen went back to claim the missing mutt.

Everyone then knew who had shot the Duffins, but the police were never charged and brought to justice.

Woeful Second World War

While Britain and Northern Ireland fought in the Second World War, the Republic of Ireland stayed neutral (well, fairly). So the German air force bombed Northern Ireland but not the Republic.

Northern Ireland had the same restrictions as mainland Britain, but with some odd Irish differences …

1 *Dad's Army* The Protestants didn't want the Catholics to join the Home Guard because that would be giving them weapons and training. After the war, they feared, the guns would be turned against them. Why worry? The Catholics didn't generally join and the Home Guard were so clumsy they managed to accidentally shoot dead their leader Colonel Hammond Smith!

2 *Evacuation* Children were supposed to leave the bomb targets – the shipyard and factory areas of Belfast. But the children didn't want to go. 17,000 were told to turn up at school, ready to be evacuated. Only 7,000 arrived.

3 *Bomb shelters* 'Every house will have a bomb shelter!' the government declared. By March 1941 only 15% had them. No wonder the bombers killed so many. In just four weeks of bombing in April 1941, the Germans had killed almost a thousand and damaged 56,000 homes. The homeless people were moved into huts – and some were still living there in 1974!

4 *Defences* All the anti-aircraft guns had been sent to mainland Britain. When the German bombers arrived they had few problems in finding their targets, dropping their bombs and getting home safely. Whose fault was it? A Northern Ireland MP had no doubts: 'The government is no good,' he said.

5 *The Troubles* The Republic of Ireland executed nine IRA members during the Second World War. But when Northern

Ireland tried to execute six IRA terrorists the government in the south objected! In the end just the terrorist leader, Tom Williams, was hanged. At his execution Catholics and Protestants squabbled outside the jail. Catholics fell to their knees and prayed while Protestants sang 'God Save the King' and 'There'll always be an England'.

EPILOGUE

How many Bloody Sundays can there be?

Most countries remember the good days of their history. The USA has 4 July for Independence Day and France has 14 June for Bastille Day when their Revolution began. The British remember Victory in Europe (VE) day.

But the Irish also remember lots of days when some actions were so horrible they call it a 'Bloody' day. Now you'd imagine there could be just seven 'Bloody' days at the most. In fact there are far more. Take 'Bloody Sunday' for example …

Bloody Sunday the first

Sunday 30 August 1913

Blood on the streets of Dublin. The workers have been on strike so the factory owners locked them out. Today the workers' leader, Big Jim Larkin, tried to speak to his supporters in Sackville Street. He slipped past the police by wearing a false beard and climbed up to the balcony of the Imperial Hotel.

The police charged into the unarmed people and hacked them down with clubs and swords. Some say six hundred people were wounded. Well, it was at least four hundred! Some of them were just passing by.

Big Jim says his job is to create unrest. I guess this bloody Sunday's work was a success!

In the 1913 disputes there were thirty separate strikes. The canal workers refused to move barges, the bricklayers refused to move bricks, the newsboys refused to move newspapers and the manure workers refused to move ... anything either.

The match workers were the only ones who could *really* claim ...

Even schoolboys at the National School in Rutland Street, Dublin went on strike! Of course you wouldn't dream of following their dreadful example, would you?

Bloody Sunday the second

Sunday 21 November 1920

What a day of murder and revenge!
It started when the Irish Republican
Brotherhood got a group of assassins
together they called the 'Gang'. They were
worried about the British spies who were
giving information to the police. So, in
the early hours of this morning, the Gang
set out to exterminate the spies. They
killed eleven of them – most of them in
their beds and many in front of their
wives and children. Three more were
wounded – and another three totally
innocent men were killed by mistake!
Of course the British were never going
to let the IRB get away with it. They
couldn't track down the Gang so they went
after the people they could get. First
they had three prisoners in Dublin Castle
shot. Then they packed soldiers into lorries
and drove into Croke Park where there
was the Gaelic football cup final being
played. They just opened fire on the

> *players and the crowd! Unbelievable!*
> *They killed a player and fourteen men*
> *and women. Sixty others were wounded*
> *or hurt in the panic.*
> *What a bloody Sunday this has been.*

Yet again, it was the innocent and the unarmed who suffered as much as the people directly involved in the hatred.

Of course the IRA got their revenge by killing another 18 at Kilmichael. Then the troops got their revenge for the killing at Kilmichael by burning down a large part of Cork a few weeks later … and so it went on.

Bloody Sunday the third

> **Sunday 10 July 1921**
>
> Belfast. Yet another Bloody Sunday
> A group of thugs who supported the
> Protestants attacked Catholics in the city
> today. They not only killed fifteen
> but they burned down over a hundred
> and sixty houses.
> Dublin has had two bloody Sundays. Let's
> hope Ulster doesn't have another.

Bloody Sunday the fourth

Sunday 30 January 1972

Derry. Ulster. There was a peaceful march through the city today. At least it was planned as a peaceful march but it didn't turn out that way.

Just last August the British government started arresting terrorist suspects. That would have been fine except the police lists they were using were out of date, and isn't it strange that 450 arrests were made and not a single Protestant was among them! No wonder the Catholics tried to march in protest. And is it any wonder the government tried to ban the march? But why did they have to send in paratroopers to stop the marchers? There was only one way it could all end, and sure enough it did. The paratroopers turned their guns and shot thirteen unarmed marchers dead.

Another bloody Sunday. How many bloody Sundays can there be?

You shouldn't be surprised to learn that the 1972 bloodshed led to revenge attacks and more bloodshed. In Dublin the Catholics reacted by burning the British Embassy to the ground ...

So, in Ulster, Protestant murder gangs set out to kill Catholics ...

So the IRA started a bombing blitz against people in crowded shopping centres.

1972 started with the killing of 13 people on Bloody Sunday ... but by the end of the year another 470 people had been killed.